My Precious Little One

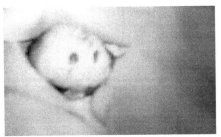

Joy Ann Sanford

Helping Those Who Have Lost a Child

By Sheila L. Sober

My Precious Little One
Helping Those Who Have Lost a Child

Unless otherwise noted, all scripture quotations are taken
from the King James Version of the Bible.

Cover design & Layout by: Cynthia D. Johnson
@www.diverseskillcenter.com

Printed in the United States of America
ISBN: **13: 978-1507573792** ISBN: **1507573790**

Table of Contents

This book is dedicated to my lovely daughter, Joy Ann Sanford, who is in Heaven,

To all the parents who have lost children, and

To the precious children who have passed on from this life:

H. Alexander P.
Christie Leann
Richard J.
Christopher M.
Emma Faith Janiczek
Jimmy S.
Shantanelle B.
Kyle Wilson Mead
Little Praise
Andrew Price Jetmore

Brad W.
Tysean T.
Candace Kate F.
James Y.
Shayne Story
Lisa H.
Akilah Johnson
Kara DePasquale
Little Bit

and the child of Carol H.
and the child of Randy Sober
and the child of
Richard and Deidre Shaw

A special thank you to all the grieving parents who have so willingly shared their comments so that others will be helped.

Introduction

Truly, losing a child is a traumatic event! It does not matter whether the child was *(1)* lost as a result of a miscarriage, a stillbirth, or a tragic accident, *(2)* died as a young child, *(3)* died as a young adult, or *(4)* died at the ruthless hands of another individual. The trauma is real! The trauma is intense!

Unfortunately, many people trying to console parents who have lost a child do not know how to do so effectively. Quite often, people are unsure of what they should say or do. In part, it may be that losing a child is such a mind boggling event for anyone to comprehend.

We just don't understand why a child has to die! It is very hard to find the right words to say for such a traumatic event as this! Consequently, many individuals end up saying or doing things that are going to be more harmful to the parents' emotional, and quite possibly, their spiritual state.

Does this mean that we should not try to console parents who have lost a child? No, it does not! It does mean, however, that we need to exercise caution in the things that we say and do around grieving parents. Additionally, we should exercise more sensitivity to the grieving parents' feelings at this time of intense sorrow.

Why must a child die? We may never truly know the answer to that question, but one thing that we can know for sure is that we have an enemy whose prime purpose is to utterly destroy us.

Therefore, when dealing with parents grieving the loss of a child, we really need discernment from the Holy Spirit concerning what we should say or do for them. As believers, Christians need to be certain that they do not become a tool for the enemy to use during this time.

Since the enemy, the devil, only has the power to do one thing, he will most definitely use that tactic. And, that one thing is the power of speaking lies. Oftentimes, these lies are mixed with facts so that one cannot distinguish the difference.

Therefore, it is vital to have discernment from the Holy Spirit and knowledge of the Word of God in such matters when helping someone through the traumatic event of losing a child.

After the initial loss of the child, the first lie that the devil will attempt to plant into the minds of the grieving parents is that *"it's God's fault."* This particular lie is as old as the Garden of Eden. Next, the devil will try to find someone who will reinforce this lie. Don't be that someone!

Oftentimes, what people say to grieving parents will get twisted up in the parents' minds by unseen forces. These unseen forces are trying to trip the parents up so that they will either turn their back on God or not come to Him at all.

If this happens, it may be many wasted years before these parents would come back to God. Even then, trusting God fully again will be a huge issue.

Therefore, it is vitally important that we do not become a tool that the enemy uses to *(1)* confirm or compound his lies, or *(2)* to invoke further blame or anger towards God.

In this book, I have attempted to expose some of these lies of the devil as well as the things that are most likely to become more damaging spiritually and emotionally for the grieving parents. Additionally, I have added things that would be most beneficial to parents during this time of sorrow.

Primarily, this book will begin with a poem that God had given to me a few years ago expressing the feelings that I had for the loss of my child. Then, the first chapter, *Joy Is Gone*, deals with my personal experience concerning the loss of my daughter, Joy.

In the remaining chapters, the book will deal with the heart of the matter – – What can I do to help? But, first, we will take a look at the things that are harmful. Then, we will take a look at the things that are beneficial.

In the last two chapters, we will deal with the range of emotions that a grieving parent could feel and\or exhibit. Lastly, we will take a look at how God is the only one that can heal this intense pain the grieving parents feel.

Hopefully, this book will help grieving parents to find peace and joy through God again. Additionally, this book will hopefully be effective in helping those desiring to minister and comfort grieving parents.

In order for this to occur, many grieving parents have relived the pain while sharing their comments with me for this book. For this, I'm truly grateful for their profound courage to face this trauma again. I pray that you have found healing through Jesus Christ our Lord.

Note: Some of the parents will be directly quoted; however, some of these grieving parents desire to remain anonymous. Also, names in bold are either personal stories or quotes people were told personally.

Disclaimer: When relating my personal experience, I will be naming certain religious denominations. None of these denominations are to be considered in a bad light. It is not my intent. However, to give a better understanding of my experience, I needed to name the particular denomination that I was attending at the time. These denominations were not responsible for what occurred to me. It was my choices and my spiritual understanding that are to blame.

Also, I would like to state that I am not a psychiatrist, a psychologist, a licensed minister, or a counselor. This book is based primarily upon personal experiences as well as relating experiences of other grieving parents. And, it is not intended for diagnosis, treatment, or replacement of other forms of treatment.

My Precious Little One Poem
By Sheila Sober

Oh, My Precious Little One,
my love for you feels so undone.
Your life on earth was for a short time.
And for this, my heart doth daily pine.

I felt you growing inside of me.
And, I long for your face to see.
Oh, My Precious Little One,
I loved you whether daughter or son.

Then, the dreadful day appeared.
It's one that many parents fear.
Your life was quickly gone:
my Life, my Joy, and my Song.

As I looked upon your face,
a mark of death was in its place.
I could not see your beautiful eyes,
nor hear your breath or sighs.

A smile I never would get to see,
or hear you ever laugh with glee,
or skip, or run, or jump,
or hear a heartbeat pump.

I would not be able to hear you bawl,
see you walk, stand, run, or crawl.
Nor would I be able to hold you close to me,
and watch you sleeping so quietly.

Forgive me for holding other babes for a space.
None of them could ever take your place.

● ● ●

I just felt so all alone,
And I wondered what it would have been like to
have brought you home.

Taking apart the nursery
was the cruelest part for me.
I was decorating it just for you.
Now, all I can do is feel blue.

Often, I wonder that first day of school,
would you cry or be cool?
Would I your hand have to hold?
Or, would you enter in quite bold?

My Precious Little One you see,
how I miss you so greatly!
I watch other children your age.
Then, I quickly become enraged.

How can this be fair? How can it be right?
I would have loved you will all of my might.
Some parents, their kids, they abuse.
Or, they don't even care if they lose.

Why, oh why, did it have to be me
to lose My Precious Little One so early?
Trying to make sense of it all,
I could only crumble and fall.

Others tried to help me through;
but, daily I saw I was missing you.
I watched other kids' growth and spurts.
Oh! How very much this loss hurts!

I miss watching you play,
graduate, and marry one day.

• • •

I often wonder what you would have been like,
meek and mild or a tough little tyke.

Birthdays, anniversaries, and holidays are cruel.
For, in my mind, I fight this duel.
I don't want to bring others down;
but yet, your joy does not me surround.

Many said it was all in God's plan,
but this I could not comprehend.
At first, I became really angry at Him.
And, I may have even dived into sin.

But, you see this was not God's handiwork.
'Cause, God don't like His children to hurt.
Only in Him do I find consolation
and the hope of my heart's restoration.

There is nothing anyone can say or do
in order to help me to get through-
except for this one thing each day-
Pray, pray, pray, and pray!

Only God can heal a broken heart
My Precious Little One.
And, He did so by showing me
that you are with His Son.
My hope is one day to see you
in Heaven.
Because now, I know you are
truly living.

Children are a gift from God above.
And, I cherish that for you
He gave me such love.

Such joy for a time you
brought to my heart;
but for a time now,
we must part.

I will see you very soon
again one day.
And, all of this pain
will melt away.

I know you would not want
me to be so sad.
But, oh! how it hurts
so very bad!

How in this life can I travel on
when I know
that you are not along?

It is only by God's grace;
And, the hope of one day
seeing your smiling face.

Although I have tried
to memorialize your name,
nothing natural
can take away the pain.

It can only come
through the Son.

Oh, how I love you
My Precious Little One!

So, I say goodbye for now,
My Precious Little One.

Joy Is Gone
Chapter 1
(Based upon author's true story)

Springtime! It was not only a time for the flowers to begin to bloom, but love also had begun to blossom in my heart for another. Just a few short months before, I had come to Wichita, Kansas to live during my senior year. Being the new kid on the block was not a new concept for me. Since we had moved a lot, I had changed schools many times before this. For me, it was another great adventure and a chance to meet new people. Little did I know, I was about to meet the first great love of my life.

His name was Doran Sanford. He was a handsome fellow and quite tall. When he smiled, it was like the sun had entered the room. Doran was one of those people who, when he woke up in the morning, would smile real big and say, *"Good Morning!"* And, it didn't matter if it was 5 a.m. or not.

Although he had had a rocky start to life, nearly dying himself as a baby, he enjoyed life to the fullest. As a result of his traumatic infancy event, he had ended up with cerebral palsy. However, he did not let this stop him. He overcame obstacles in his life. I looked up to him for this, as I do with all those who have great obstacles to overcome. Soon, I would be facing one of my hugest obstacles in my life - the death of a child.

Doran attended the same church that I did, and he was the church bus driver. I was one of the passengers on that bus. We were introduced by someone we both knew and loved greatly. Doran was now twenty-nine years of age and not yet married. I was only seventeen and not quite 5 ft. tall. However, our age and height differences to us did not matter. It was not long before we began to date and eventually to discuss marriage. Our plans were to be married in August sometime after my 18th birthday.

Excited, I could hardly contain the news! I could not wait to share it with my new friends! Seventeen, and I felt like I had the world whipped by the tail! I was all grown up now because I was getting married! Just a few more months away, and I would be free to be my own person. I would get to be my own boss!

Finally, it was time for school. Now, all I had to do was to wait for that lunch bell to ring!

When it did, I rushed into the lunch room and found my friends sitting at the long metal bench and table ready to eat their lunch. Quickly and excitedly, I was able to finally share the news of my pending nuptials with them. They were very happy for me.

Shortly after graduation, I had plans to go to a Bible college. I already had earned two small scholarships through the Word of Life program. I obtained these scholarships by memorizing over 100 verses of Scripture and passing their exam. Additionally, I felt like God had called me to the mission field when I was sixteen years of age. Getting married was about to change these plans.

Later that spring, in early April, I was told that after I got married I would be put on birth control. There was no way this was going to happen! I wanted children desperately, and no one was going to tell me what to do after I got married!

So, despite my spiritual beliefs and much internal conflict, I went out and purposefully got pregnant. Little did I know how much I had started down a wrong road, or the anguish lying ahead for me.

Given my upbringing in a fundamentalist Baptist Church, I knew the Scriptures well.

Since I had compromised my spiritual beliefs, the emotional and spiritual battle was on.

Attempting to rationalize the pregnancy in my mind, I told myself that getting pregnant was all right since we were getting married. But was it? No, it did not make it right.

At first, I did not realize that I had succeeded in getting pregnant. I just had a few mornings of nausea, but that was it. Not long after, a family member noticed and told me that she knew that I was pregnant. No test was done yet or would be until much later. She just knew.

Consequently, the decision was made to push the wedding up to June, before my 18th birthday, and before I would begin to show. This would save the family much embarrassment.

School was another matter. Getting through the last few months of high school was very difficult. I remember such extreme fatigue. I was so afraid that I was going to fall asleep in class and get into trouble. However, I did manage to finish. And, I finished with honors.

During the next few months, preparing for the wedding was like a whirlwind. Preparations ensued up until the very last minute.

Since the wedding would be taking place two weeks after graduation, most of my family would not be able to get off of work to attend both events. So, I had very few attend my graduation.

It was just as well. For, a very embarrassing situation occurred. Five minutes before we were to start the procession, I had somehow split both side seams all the way down. Hurriedly, the teachers grabbed safety pins and pinned my gown back together just in time for me to march with the rest of the graduating class.

Shortly after graduation, I finally went to the Driver's Bureau and got my drivers license. If I was going to help my husband drive on our honeymoon, I was going to need it. And, I found out on my honeymoon later just how much that I needed to be doing the driving. Doran had a problem with falling asleep at the wheel. I found this out after being awakened while on the honeymoon trip when he fell asleep and hit some construction cones.

Back to my wedding day, I remember sitting in the roller rink with my family making the rice bags. We were at the roller rink because it was my cousin's birthday. Although I was pregnant, I still wanted to roller skate. And, I did too.

One of my favorite memories was a comment that was made. When I was preparing to go out on the floor, I was told, *"If you fall down and break your leg, we will carry you down the aisle."* We all had a great laugh, and it went well. I roller skated without incident.

Later that evening, on June 9, 1984, we pulled up to a small Baptist Church for the wedding. My dress had arrived at the last minute. But, it was very beautiful and handmade. The candelabrum was all lit up. And, my husband - to - be was already waiting downstairs in the pastor's office. It was a very beautiful wedding.

After the wedding, some of the family followed us all the way out to the Haysville rodeo grounds to the mobile home where my husband and I would be living. We visited for a while, and then they left. The next day, Doran and I set off for our honeymoon trip.

All was going well with the pregnancy until the honeymoon trip. Our plans were to go to Indiana to visit family, then Illinois to visit family, and finally to the Wisconsin Dells. The latter was one of my favorite childhood vacation spots.

However, while in Indiana, we contracted the flu bug. As soon as we were well enough to travel, we went on to Illinois and then to Wisconsin. Again, I was told by a different family member there in Illinois that I was pregnant without tests still yet having been done. What led her to this conclusion? I had gotten up in the middle of the night to eat. Later, after the honeymoon, I finally got a pregnancy test done. It came back positive.

After returning home, things began to normalize somewhat. I was beginning to settle into my new role as a wife and soon - to - be mother. Doran treated me like I was queen. In his eyes, it seemed like I could do no wrong. Truly, he knew how to cherish a woman. Doran worked hard for a construction company. And, it was our job to keep the rodeo grounds mowed.

Unfortunately, I was not quite used to all of the responsibility that an adult has. I had to grow up quickly. I was told many years later that at the age of seventeen that I had the emotional maturity of a twelve-year-old. Looking back, I can see that. Not understanding financial matters, I caused my husband and myself great debt. This occurred because my husband had handed the financial matters over to me. However, we were able to get some things for the baby and the nursery.

Slowly, but surely, the second bedroom of the trailer was beginning to look like a nursery. It would not be long now!

During my pregnancy, one of my funniest memories occurred during one of our doctor's visits. My husband and I were told, at first, by the doctor, that he thought we would have twins. This made my husband so nervous. He was barely prepared for one let alone two babies. His body reacted to the shock of this by breaking out in hives. Later, we found out by the doctor that there was only one child. Boy, my husband was relieved.

Additionally, during my pregnancy, I had gained quite a bit of weight in three months time. But the doctor did not seem concerned. Later, I would find out that the doctor only liked to deliver 10 pound babies.

In the following months of my pregnancy, I spent a lot of time alone at home while my husband worked. The enemy, the devil, began to torment my mind with fear. Through my sin, I had opened the door for him to operate.

Now, fear was driving me not to want the baby anymore. I did some crazy things; however, it was not something that would hurt the child without harming me. I never took anything internally. The fear was driving me to attempt suicide by other means. Since I did not really want to die, I never quite took it far enough to cause any damage to myself or the baby. I was not aware that it was a spiritual battle that was ensuing; nor, did I know how to fight it.

Eventually, I remembered my spiritual upbringing. So, I decided to return to church. But, I did not go back to the Baptist church. I had heard that others had switched their beliefs from Baptist to Pentecostal. So, I decided to try this denomination, and I found a Pentecostal church in Wichita to attend. Quickly, I became active in the church. I helped in the nursery and sang in the choir.

While attending there, I learned about the baptism of the Holy Ghost with the evidence of speaking in tongues. For the first time in my life, I desired this baptism.

Now, it was about the seventh month of my pregnancy. My doctor wanted to perform a fasting glucose tolerance test. Since diabetes runs heavy in my family, he felt I had a predisposition to gestational diabetes. Although the test came back normal, I would later feel that this had an impact upon my baby. At this point, the baby was still in the breech position.

As a side note, I have one piece of advice for anybody going through this test. Do not go to a fast food restaurant after the test is over! Enough said!

Well, as time passed, my mind had settled down. I had finally come to terms with being pregnant and began to enjoy it. Now, I longed to love and hold our baby. I had already gone into protection mode for our child.

One day, while walking down the long winding pathway around the rodeo grounds, we were followed by our two Pitbull\German Shepherd puppies. Additionally, we had a cat that had a litter of kittens. This cat also began to follow behind.

Unfortunately, the two puppies noticed. They began to chase the cat. She dashed up the light pole for safety. The cat watched and waited for the dogs to leave. So, we called the dogs to us. They turned and started towards us.

Just then, the cat thought it was safe, and scurried down the pole. Upon the cat hitting the ground, the puppies heard and twisted around quickly. They gave chase. Catching the mother cat, they began to play tug-of-war. We were too far away to help her. All we could do was to scream at the dogs to stop! It was too late.

When the puppies killed the mother cat, I immediately became fearful for our baby. I had heard all the stories about Pitbull dogs once they had tasted blood. If they would do that to a cat, what would they do to a small infant?

Therefore, I felt we had no choice but to take them to the pound and have the puppies put to sleep. I hated doing this. Upon returning home, we looked for the baby kittens. We could only find two live ones from the litter. Later, we found them homes.

After a short while, things began to settle down again. Spiritually, I had begun to pray more now that I had a lot of time to myself.

Soon, it was early December. It would not be much longer before the child would be born. And, Christmas was just around the corner! I had rededicated my life to Lord. And, I was in the process of changing denominations from a fundamental Baptist upbringing to a Pentecostal belief.

At this time, I was learning how one can hear from God when praying. I thought I was praying in the Spirit, but I was not. This would not occur until much later for real. Also, during this time of prayer, I believed that God had told me that I was going to have a healthy baby boy, and he would arrive earlier than expected.

However, lacking the understanding of spiritual things in this area, I had been deceived by the enemy. Praying in the Spirit, and God speaking things to you is real; but, one also needs to know the difference between the voices that they hear whether it be from God or not. I did not have this discernment yet. I was about to find this out.

Shortly after the dog incident, my husband's insurance required me to begin Lamaze classes. I had learned a lot of things. When having abdominal pain, sometimes I still use the breathing techniques and effleurage that I had learned during Lamaze class.

On December 13th, our class was scheduled to tour the hospital Maternity Ward. This is one trip that I would not be taking with the class.

On December 7th, the phone rang.

Wondering who it could be, I went to answer it.

"Hello, Sanford residence."

"Is this Sheila Sanford?" the caller asked.

"Yes," I answered.

"Sheila, I'm calling to let you know that the doctor has to cancel your appointment for today. Right now, he is delivering someone's baby. Would you like to see another doctor in the office or wait until Monday to see your regular doctor?" the receptionist asked.

"I think I will wait till Monday. I would rather my regular doctor see me," I answered.

Since I had felt fine and saw no reason not to wait, I rescheduled for Monday. However, this was the wrong decision.

Over the weekend, every time that I ate something, my stomach felt as hard as a rock. Being young and unlearned about pregnancy, I did not realize anything was wrong with the baby. I just thought it was strange that food was affecting me that way.

On Monday, December 10th, I went to see the doctor as scheduled. After a few minutes, the doctor had a puzzled look on his face. He gently told me that he could not detect the baby's heartbeat at this time. He wanted to make sure the baby was not under stress. So, he wanted me to go the next day to the hospital and have a stress test done.

Naïvely, I still did not sense that anything was seriously wrong. I told the doctor that I would go for the test the next day.

So, on Tuesday, December 11th, I went to St. Francis Hospital for a stress test. However, I still did not think anything was really wrong with the baby. I still had the utmost trust in the medical profession. I almost idolized them. If anything was wrong, they would be able to fix it. Right? Wrong! Medical personnel are not God! They can do what they know to do, but they are limited at some point.

Walking into the hospital, I still did not fear. After I had checked in, I went up to the Maternity Ward. The nurse had me change, and I climbed into the hospital bed. She began to wrap something around my stomach that had long lines leading back to a big machine.

Shortly after, my doctor came into the room. Even though it was a cold winter day, the room was very brightly lit. The doctor looked at the monitor, and without saying a word, he left the room.

Having spent years as a people watcher, I began to notice the doctor speaking with different people. They were going in and out of the room. Yet, no one was saying a word to me.

The medical staff was whispering amongst themselves. However, one nurse continued to stay with me. For the first time, I began to sense something might be wrong.

I turned my head towards the nurse and asked, *"What's going on?"*

"You mean you don't know! Your baby is dead!" the nurse curtly replied.

I felt like I had just been run over by a semi truck. How could this be happening? How could it be happening to us, and our baby?

I just burst into tears and sobbed for a long time. My husband held me and cried with me. Joy was gone. Not only the baby, but also my inner joy had gone. I felt like I would never get it back.

Finally, the doctor solemnly entered the room. I briefly composed myself to hear what he had to say.

"Sheila, during the stress test, unfortunately we could not detect a heartbeat. This means that your baby has died. I'm sorry. Now, what I would like to do is to induce labor and deliver it naturally."

All I could do was just nod in agreement. I was still in such a state of shock. I could not believe this was happening! My world had just crumbled all around me. I felt as if I were sitting in a heap of ashes. Why, oh why, did this have to happen to us?

After the nurse had inserted the IV, every few hours the resident doctor, or my doctor, would come in to check for dilation.

Meanwhile, one of the resident doctors that came in and checked me for dilation said, *"I'm sorry you lost your baby. But, you are young and healthy enough. You've got plenty of time to have more kids."* This just upset me all the more. Another child could not replace this one or take away the pain and sorrow that I was feeling.

As time passed, my husband had stayed by my side except to call family with the news. It was not long before his family and some of my family had arrived at the hospital to offer their condolences.

After two days of IV therapy to try to induce labor, there was still no dilation. The doctor decided to unhook me from the IV, but he decided to leave the heparin lock in place. That night, I was allowed to go home to be with family. However, I was returned to the hospital the next day.

On Thursday, December 13th, I returned to the hospital Maternity Ward. I was hooked back up to the IV. After several hours and still no dilation, the doctor entered the room; and, he gave me three choices:

- Carry the baby to term and risk hemorrhaging to death.
- Continue trying to induce labor and deliver naturally.
- Or, have a C-Section and remove the baby. This had its own set of risks.

I was in such shock and unable to speak. I was terrified of all three choices. I did not know what to do! I could not physically answer the doctor. Up to this point in my life, I had never had surgery.

To add to the shock, the doctor had to know before 10 p.m., as he was going to be leaving for San Salvador and be gone for a week.

Consequently, the decision fell upon my husband's shoulders. Doran, my husband, chose the C-Section option with the permission to be in the operating room. Permission was granted. Also, I asked to be allowed to have my focal point Teddy Bear that I was using for Lamaze in the operating room. Permission was granted for that as well.

Somewhere around 10 p.m., I was wheeled into the operating room with my husband by my side and my Teddy Bear in my hands. They had me get up on the gurney and lay on my left side. Ironically, I had to lie in almost a fetal position.

The anesthesiologist put some numbing stuff on my back. I began to do my Lamaze breathing and focused on my Teddy Bear while the anesthesiologist injected a needle into my spine. As the fluid began to flow, I slowly became numb from the chest down. To add to the shock of losing a child, I was in shock that I was going to be awake for the surgery! This further terrified me!

Eventually, they rolled me over onto my back with my arms stretched out to the sides and placed upon armrests. Draped high above my chest and coming down to it was a cloth so that I could not see what was going on. An oxygen mask was placed on my face, and a blood pressure cuff was attached to my left arm. Off to my left, was the anesthesiologist. And, up against the wall, my husband stood.

"Sheila, you may feel some pressure when we cut into you. But, you should not feel any pain," the doctor said. I was feeling pain, but it just wasn't physical.

All of a sudden, I became panicky! It was as if I could not breathe! I remember grabbing the oxygen mask and pulling it from off of my face.

"I can't breathe!" I cried out. My face became all itchy around my mouth like I was growing facial hair. My arms, which still had feeling, began to tremble. Later, I was told that my blood pressure was all over the place. And, I found out that I must have been slightly allergic to the morphine.

The anesthesiologist tried to reassure me, and he put the oxygen mask back on my face. The doctor let me know that I might feel some pulling when they repositioned my organs. Not realizing that they were almost done, I asked him when they were going to begin.

"We're all done. All we have to do is stitch you up," the doctor said.

Later, the cause of my daughter's death was revealed to me. It was the umbilical cord; however, it was a strange occurrence how it had happened the doctor told me. The umbilical cord was wrapped around the baby's <u>ankle</u> which had pinched off the oxygen supply to the baby.

For this reason, years later, I thought the glucose test may have had something to do with my baby's loss. The baby was breech, and maybe the glucose excited her enough that she started turning and got caught up in the cord. I was of a short stature, just under 5 foot; and, the baby was already around 22 inches in length and 5 pounds.

After the surgery, I was taken back to the recovery room. My husband was also allowed in there with me. I asked the nurse if I could hold my baby. Very soon after, the nurse brought in this bundle wrapped in a pink blanket. She placed the baby in my arms. I just stared down at her. I noticed her cute little mouth, and how her eyes just appeared as if she were sleeping. I stroked her soft, black hair gently.

She had the softest, thickest, blackest hair! I remember having mixed emotions. I was happy that we had such a beautiful daughter. But, I was sad that she would never open her eyes; and, I would never get to hear her cry.

A little while later, I handed her back to the nurse. I really wish that they had taken the picture of her while I was holding her. Instead, it must have been quite a while later. For in the photo, you can already see the decay. I did not see this when I had held her.

Because the weather had turned to snow, some people could not get there the night of my surgery. Later, they would arrive. One person, when she was able to finally get there, had also just started attending a Pentecostal church. She was zealous for the Lord! However, she made a very hurtful comment to me.

She said, *"If you had not allowed them to take the baby yet, God could have raised her from the dead."*

Immediately, I felt like I was to blame. Now, I felt like I had done something - not once, not twice, but now three times to cause the death of my child.

Furthermore, I had great fear that I would miss my baby's funeral because of the hospitalization. The family and my husband were handling all the details; but, they let me know what was going on. However, one thing that I wanted was an open casket, but the mortician advised against it. Baby Joy was buried in a white pillowed casket. It was perfect and would have been my choice.

Baby Joy would be buried about three hours away from where we lived. My husband and I could not afford a burial plot, and one of the family members had a plot that had a baby in the first half of it. They allowed Doran and I to put Baby Joy in the other half of the plot.

Although financially this helped, it hurt emotionally because I could not easily go and visit the grave any time that I wanted. This was due to financial constraints.

Additionally, our daughter only had a temporary plate. We could never afford a headstone. To this day, one is not there. Where would I tell them to put it now? Over the years, I had made a couple of visits, but it was difficult to tell exactly where Baby Joy was. However, I do know where our daughter is now—in heaven with Jesus!

Although losing a child is quite an emotional blow, one of the greatest moments that I had was when I was released from the hospital, and there was a time of laughter. This occurred before the funeral.

Upon release from the hospital, my family decided that we would go out to eat. My dad was doing the driving. With staples in my stomach, it seemed like my dad went down the bumpiest road ever in town. It was made entirely of bricks.

Finally, we reached the diner. As we sat down in the booth and looked at our menus, the waitress appeared.

"May I take your order, please?" she asked.

Looking at the menu that had some misprints on it, my mom gave her order. I cannot recall her choice of meat, but my mother read the side dish that she wanted as it was printed.

● ● ●

"And, I will have the mashed bashed fried rice," my mother stated. We all just busted out laughing. If it had been written correctly, the choices would have been mashed potatoes, bashed potatoes, or fried rice.

For me, it kind of hurt to laugh because of the staples; but, it made me feel really good to laugh.

The jocularity continued. We had all ordered fruit Jell-O for dessert. Unfortunately, the fruit was a scarcity. My dad went on and on about how he did not have any fruit in his fruit Jell-O.

"I guess this is fruit Jell-O. I don't see any fruit. Hey! You got fruit! I didn't get any fruit in my fruit Jell-O!" my dad exclaimed while pointing to the different Jell-O's. I thought I was going to bust out my stitches from laughing so hard. Although the laughter hurt physically, it was very good for me. Unfortunately, it did not replace the lost joy in my heart.

A few days later, my staples were removed; and, I received butterfly strips that I had to wear for a week. At this time, my parents got permission for me to travel. We drove for 14 hours to see my grandmother that Doran and I had just seen on our honeymoon. We ended up staying a week. It was one of my favorite places to go.

After the week was up, my parents drove all the way home. Then, they put Doran and I on a short flight home. This plane was a little twin -

prop plane. I had never flown before. I was a little apprehensive about getting on the plane.

It had already been raining all day. But, the flight was only supposed to last an hour. There were only three souls on board besides the pilot and copilot. I glanced around the interior of the plane, and I quickly realized that there were no bathrooms on board!

On the way home, we hit so much turbulence. This terrified me! It was right after the New Year, and our final destination was receiving ice not rain! We were one of the last flights in.

Since I had never flown before, this was an experience that created mixed emotions. I was scared; yet, I felt at peace. The other passenger was about as young as I, or younger, and she did not seem scared. However, after the flight and landing on ice, I decided that I never wanted to fly again! Eventually, I did. But, it was thirty years later.

Sometime, shortly after the trip, the hard part really began. Loneliness began to set in. Since we lived in the country, we did not get many visitors. I do not recollect even the church people coming by. Family was scattered all over and had to go home to their jobs. And, I had no close friendships at this time. I had been left alone to grieve and to try to figure things out myself.

Instead of turning to God, I ran from God. Several times I attempted to go back to church. I even tried to hold the babies there. But, it became too difficult for me to deal with emotionally. Consequently, I left the church.

As a result, my life only continued to decline spiritually and emotionally. More of this will be explained in later chapters. Eventually, I had entered into total rebellion against God. It would be almost sixteen years before I would truly come back to God.

During the time of the loss, and for many years after, some of the things said, done, or not done actually had made me angrier at God. It precipitated my turning away from Him instead of to Him. What you do or say during this time does matter a whole lot.

Eventually, I did give my heart back to God. And, I did get baptized in the Holy Spirit with the evidence of speaking in tongues. It was not until I truly turned to God that I found the peace, joy, and healing that I so desperately needed.

Whatever you say or do to help someone through this kind of a loss, be sure to point them to Jesus. For, He can fully understand what it means to be brokenhearted. And, He was sent and anointed to heal those who have a broken heart.

If you're reading this book, and you have just lost a child, turn to Him. Only Jesus can understand and heal your broken heart.

16 Things Not To Say or Do

Don't Say,
"It's God's Will."
Chapter 2

"Lo, children are an heritage of the Lord: and the fruit of the womb is his reward." **Psalm 127:3 (KJV)**

"Every good gift and every perfect gift is from above, and cometh down from the Father of lights, with whom is no variableness, neither shadow of turning."
James 1:17 (KJV)

Telling someone that the death of their child is God's will is very wrong. Unfortunately, the saying is usually found in Christian circles. Although I cannot recollect who or when this was said to me concerning the death of my child, I am almost certain that it was.

When I began to write things that people should not say to grieving parents, this was one of the first things that came out of my heart. In fact, it began to make me a little angry. I may not remember someone saying this to me, especially if it was stated while I was still in a state of shock.

Many years later, however, I remember someone stating something similar concerning the will of God for me to have a spouse. I still greatly desired to have children and believed God for them. However, at the time, I was single again. As I recall, a fellow brother in Christ told me that maybe it wasn't God's will for me to have a spouse.

● ● ●

Just prior to this, I remember hearing a message about a father's blessing that occurred many times in the Old Testament. The minister had stated that fathers should bless their children. So, when my dad came to visit, I asked him to pray a blessing over me. Although I was looking for work at the time, his prayer of blessing for me was for a Godly spouse.

Therefore, I disagreed with the Christian brother who told me that it was possibly not God's will for me to have a husband. Basically, I told him, *"If I was going to have children, I had to have a husband. It would not be God's will for me to do so out of wedlock."*

One year later, I was married to my current husband. And, we had too many things occur that confirmed that we were to be married. So, we knew without a shadow of a doubt, it was the will of God for us to be married.

Unfortunately, we do not have any children, but I have a better understanding of what kind of children God will let us have. It may not be God's will for me to have children now in the natural, but instead, it is His will for me to have spiritual children by giving birth to ministries that will eventually be instrumental in people coming to Jesus or growing in Christ.

Although it may not be God's will for me to have any more children in the natural at this point in my life, it was **Not** God's will for me to lose my child that I did have. And, telling me so was not only hurtful but very wrong!

• • •

Similarly, I know that others have been told that it was God's will when they had lost a child. Following is one person's story that was repeatedly told this.

"[We are told that all the time when any death occurs. My husband died when I was 22, and he was 23. It was God's will, a part of God's plan. God has a reason, etc. etc. When I remarried, and we lost our baby by miscarriage, I heard the same words.

When my husband died, and I heard those words from my father (a minister), my pastor, and several deeply religious friends.... I became very angry at God. Why would His plan bring this incredible love into my life only to take him away? Why would He "plan" for Tom to die in such a violent way? How could I love and serve a Father who could cause such pain and heartache? If that was who God was, I wanted nothing to do with His "plan".

Thankfully, in the years that passed, I made my peace with God and no longer believe it was part of His plan. I believe He knew what would happen that day, but I do not believe it was by His hand that Tom died.

I remarried and lost my baby at 11 weeks. We had gone through fertility treatments just to get pregnant. When people said it was God's will, I again questioned the God I served. How could God grant the deepest desire of my heart only to take him away? Why was I not worthy to carry my baby and be his mother? Why was God's plan one of punishment and heartache?

It's been 25 years since Tom died... 10 years since my baby died. I now serve God fully and completely, believing that God is a God of comfort. I believe He knows the road that lies ahead of me which will include both happiness and heartache. I do not believe He plans to bring His children pain, but He is here to offer comfort and peace as we face life's heartaches.

I believe God is a God of love and of peace, and in His arms I will find comfort throughout my journey through this life.]" **Sharon Story**

In this chapter, I will attempt to show that losing a child to death is not God's will.

Only God Knows His Will For People's Lives

Who are we to say that we know God's will for someone's life? Most people don't even know God's will for their own lives. Also, when a person says something like that, it makes it sound like only they have a secret line to God that no one else can have.

Sometimes, when people say this, it is stemming from a place of pride or judgment. God does tell other people things sometimes about people, but He will also confirm it with the individual in their spirit. And, it would be hard pressed probably to find a parent who has ever lost a child to state that he/she felt in their spirit that it was God's will. However, a few grieving parents do accept this belief. For some believers, it is how they have been able to cope with the loss.

God Does Not Change

"Jesus Christ the same yesterday, and to day, and for ever." **Hebrews 13:8 (KJV)**

Two other reasons that it is **not** God's will for a child to die are found in scripture:

❖ The command to *"... be fruitful, and multiply,...."* in **Genesis 1:28 (KJV)**

and

❖ The fact that God said *"Lo, children are an heritage of the Lord: and the fruit of the womb is his reward."* **Psalm 127:3 (KJV)**

God does not change. His commandments are from the foundation of the earth and are still ongoing today. Otherwise, people would not be still capable of having children. Additionally, God is one who wants to reward His children. God is a keeper of His promises.

God Does Not Tempt Man With Evil

One of the worst things that could ever be said to a grieving parent, or to anyone grieving a loss period, is that it is God's will for that person to have died.

This particular comment directly attributes blame upon God for the damage and hurt that has come upon that family. The person stating this has a wrong perception of God's character, and they are being used by the enemy to pass that incorrect perception of God on. Therefore, this statement is wrong indeed!

Recently, I heard a message by **Reverend Diane Maxwell** that explains it much better. Her message is called *The Manna Principle*. Below is an excerpt of that message.

"*[In **Exodus 16:3**], they had a perception of God that was totally opposite of the character and the nature of the Lord.... [**Exodus 16:4**] is known amongst the Jewish people as what's called The Manna Principle. And, this is a principle that you will find over, and over, and over in the Old Testament Writings....*

Now, notice, that God did not respond to their mumblings and grumblings.... He said, 'I will rain bread from Heaven for you.' In other words, I will meet your need....The Lord instructed them to gather one day's portion. And, He said that, '[I am going to do this so that I can test them—if they will hear me, if they will obey me.]'

In verse 5, and on the sixth day, they shall prepare to bring in twice as much. This is the double portion.... Now, there is a couple of things that I want to point out to you here. ... God was giving them bread according to each person, according to their portion, to test them.

Notice that God tested them with blessing.... [In verse 31, with the manna,]... God was showing them that He is the sweetness. He is the provision. He is the one who will provide nutrition for our bodies.... God was teaching them that they could depend on Him....

Jesus said, '[I am the Bread from Heaven.]' And He said, '[whoever comes to me will never thirst again, will never get hungry again.]' He will provide whatever it is that you need....We can turn to Him, and He will provide for us. He will sustain us.... In ancient Jewish wisdom, it says that the manna would be to them whatever they wanted it to be....

He wanted them to listen and to obey simple instructions.... So, I want you to understand that God does not test us, you know, when we mess up. He doesn't punish us. In our day, and in our time, Jesus took all of our punishment.

Now, we can get out from underneath the blessing of God, and things can happen. But here, He is showing them if you will love me, if you will honour me, you will hear and hearken unto my voice, you will be blessed.... He tested us through the blessing. He didn't test us or test them through hardship, through difficulty, through sickness, through disease.

The test came from the blessing. That if they would do, if they would hear and do what He says; and, they will turn; and, they will honour Him and bless Him, it takes all the pressure off....

• • •

The test is of our faithfulness. The test is whether we will pass on the blessing.... Our perception of God, right or wrong, will determine the measure and the level of how we experience Him, how much of His presence that we experience, how much of the blessing of God that we experience, whether we're healed in our bodies or not, whether our families are together.

All of it depends on our perception.... God was working with them trying to change their perception. And, He showed them mighty miracles all through these years....

Miracles will not determine faithfulness.... They will not build into us what we need to be faithful. Thankfulness, gratefulness, and worship before God is what will determine our faithfulness.

'[For our God, He is good always.]' **[Deuteronomy 6:24]** *What a change in perception.... And, because they learned the Manna Principle, they learned that it's the time that God blesses them—that's the test.*

Sickness and disease is not the test. It's straight from the pit of Hell. Poverty, lack, debt, defeat, failure is not the test. The test is the blessing....The devil has totally rough shod the church in seeing the love of God. And, that's what we need more than anything....

You know, we struggle with the issue of healing. 'Well, if it's God's will?' If it wasn't God's will, Jesus wouldn't have gone to the cross.... We just saw in Deuteronomy they went from just enough, just enough for their family, to being abundantly blessed.

What is the test? To honour God, and don't forget Him. Thankfulness.... We must become developed in praising God in our pain.... You don't praise God for the pain. You praise God in the pain. And, God removes the pain because you bless Him." **Rev. Diane Maxwell**

So, as you can see, stating that it is the will of God for someone's child to die is a misrepresentation of the character and nature of God. He is **NOT** the one who has done this horrendous thing. He is **NOT** the one who is punishing or testing the parents with evil.

Furthermore, many grieving parents are already in the throes of questioning God concerning why this is happening to them. When you make this particular comment to them, it reinforces in their minds the lie of the enemy that God had something against them. In turn, this can tempt an individual to want to run from God and maybe ultimately headlong into sin.

The blame game is as old as the Garden of Eden. It is a trick that the enemy uses. He knows that if you are busy blaming God, you won't run to Him.

Additionally, Scripture shows us in the above verse, **James 1:17**, that good things come from God our Heavenly Father. In a few verses before that, we see that God does not tempt man with evil.

"Let no man say when he is tempted, I am tempted of God: for God cannot be tempted with evil, neither tempteth he any man:"
James 1:13 (KJV)

Although this passage is talking about temptation to sin, the same word tempt here can also mean *"... to try, make trial of, test: for the purpose of ascertaining his quality, or what he thinks, or how he will behave himself...."*
(Blue Letter Bible—Strong's Greek Lexicon)

God does not need to tempt or test us with bad things to see how we will come through it, to see if we are going to sin or not. He is omniscient. Thus, God already knows our hearts. He already knows what we would do in a given situation. God is not an evil God that will go and take your child from you just to see what you will do? He does not want to cause his children pain. That is **not** His will!

Well, what about Abraham and Isaac, you may ask? If you remember, God did not take Abraham's child from him. He allowed his child to live. Abraham's test was a test for an act of obedience by faith. Abraham's child was alive at the time the commandment came. It is similar to the rich young ruler who did not want to give up all of his possessions to follow God.

Abraham's test was a test to see if he was willing to give up his son. God was not going to kill the child. Abraham knew and believed that.

He knew that even if he had to go through with it, God would raise Isaac up. He knew that God did not relinquish on His promises. Isaac was the promised son. His was a test of faith, obedience, and willingness. It was not a trial sent his way after the fact to see if he would stay true to God.

When someone says that it is God's will, the grieving parents often wonder why God would want to test them with something so painful as ripping their child from their home and their lives. These parents did not lose their child of their own free will. The child was taken from them.

Therefore, it is **NOT** a test sent from God, nor is it God's will for them to have lost the child. The tempter, the devil, came and killed their child in order to cause them to turn away from God.

The Bible is very clear who the tempter is. In **Matthew 4:1 – 3**, we can clearly see that the tempter is the devil. In **John 10:10 (KJV)**, Jesus said, *"The thief cometh not, but for to steal, and to kill, and to destroy: I am come that they might have life, and that they might have it more abundantly."*

As you can see in this verse, the devil's intentions are destructive. God's intentions are life and one more abundantly. God would not intentionally put something in our path to cause us to stumble and fall. So, how could it be God's will for someone to lose a child? It can't!

Scripture Reveals God's Will For Our Lives

Following are some Scripture verses that show what God's will **IS** for us. These are the things that He desires for us.

To Heal Us
*"And Jesus saith unto him, I **will** come and heal him."* **Matthew 8:7 (KJV)**

*"Who his own self bare our sins in his own body on the tree, that we, being dead to sins, should live unto righteousness: **by whose stripes ye were healed**."* **I Peter 2:24 (KJV)**

To Give Mercy
*"But go ye and learn what that meaneth, I **will** have mercy, and not sacrifice: for I am not come to call the righteous, but sinners to repentance."* **Matthew 9:13 (KJV)**

*"Therefore hath he mercy on whom he **will** have mercy, and whom he will he hardeneth."* **Romans 9:18 (KJV)**

"For God hath concluded them all in unbelief, that he might have mercy upon all." **Romans 11:32 (KJV)**

To Give Rest
*"Come unto me, all ye that labour and are heavy laden, and I **will** give you rest."*
Matthew 11:28 (KJV)

To Save So None Would Perish
*"Even so it is **not the will** of your Father which is in heaven, that one of these little ones should perish."* **Matthew 18:14 (KJV)**

To Call To Repentance
*"The Lord is not slack concerning his promise, as some men count slackness; but is longsuffering to us-ward, **not willing** that any should perish, but that all should come to repentance."* **2 Peter 3:9 (KJV)**

*"For godly sorrow worketh **repentance** to salvation not to be repented of: but the sorrow of the world worketh **death**."*
2 Corinthians 7:10 (KJV)

To Be Cleansed
*"And there came a leper to him, beseeching him, and kneeling down to him, and saying unto him, If thou wilt, thou canst make me clean. And Jesus, moved with compassion, put forth his hand, and touched him, and saith unto him, I **will**; be thou clean. And, as soon as he had spoken, immediately the leprosy departed from him, and he was cleansed."*
Mark 1:40 – 42 (KJV)

*"If we confess our sins, he is faithful and just to forgive us our sins, and to **cleanse** us from all unrighteousness."* **I John 1:9 (KJV)**

To Have Peace And Goodwill
"Glory to God in the highest, and on earth ***peace, good will toward men.*** *"*
Luke 2:14 (KJV)

To Give Good Gifts To His Children (Holy Spirit)

"If ye then, being evil, know how to give good gifts unto your children: how much more shall your heavenly Father give the Holy Spirit to them that ask him?" **Luke 11:13 (KJV)**

"Every good gift and every perfect gift is from above, and cometh down from the Father of lights, with whom is no variableness, neither shadow of turning." **James 1: 17 (KJV)**

To Raise The Dead
"Then answered Jesus and said unto them, Verily, verily, I say unto you, The Son can do nothing of himself, but what he seeth the Father do: for what things soever he doeth, these also doeth the Son likewise.

For the Father loveth the Son, and sheweth him all things that himself doeth: and he will shew him greater works than these, that ye may marvel.

For as the Father raiseth up the dead, and quickeneth them; even so the Son quickeneth whom he ***will.***

For the Father judgeth no man, but hath committed all judgment unto the Son:

That all men should honour the Son, even as they honour the Father. He that honoureth not the Son honoureth not the Father which hath sent him.

Verily, verily, I say unto you, He that heareth my word, and believeth on him that sent me, hath everlasting life, and shall not come into condemnation; but is passed from death unto life.

Verily, verily, I say unto you, The hour is coming, and now is, when the dead shall hear the voice of the Son of God: and they that hear shall live.

For as the Father hath life in himself; so hath he given to the Son to have life in himself;

And hath given him authority to execute judgment also, because he is the Son of man.

Marvel not at this: for the hour is coming, in the which all that are in the graves shall hear his voice,

And shall come forth; they that have done good, unto the resurrection of life; and they that have done evil, unto the resurrection of damnation.

*I can of mine own self do nothing: as I hear, I judge: and my judgment is just; because I seek not mine own will, but the **will** of the Father which hath sent me."* **John 5:19 – 30 (KJV)**

*"And this is the **will** of him that sent me, that every one which seeth the Son, and believeth on him, may have everlasting life: and I **will** raise him up at the last day."* **John 6:40 (KJV)**

"But I would not have you to be ignorant, brethren, concerning them which are asleep, that ye sorrow not, even as others which have no hope.

*For if we believe that Jesus died and rose again, even so them also which sleep in Jesus **will** God bring with him.*

For this we say unto you by the word of the Lord, that we which are alive and remain unto the coming of the Lord shall not prevent them which are asleep.

*For the Lord himself shall descend from heaven with a shout, with the voice of the archangel, and with the trump of God: and the dead in Christ **shall rise** first:*

Then we which are alive and remain shall be caught up together with them in the clouds to meet the Lord in the air: and so shall we ever be with the Lord.

Wherefore comfort one another with these words."
I Thessalonians 4:13 – 18 (KJV)

To Lose None Who Come To Jesus
*"And this is the Father's **will** which hath sent me, that of all which he hath given me I should*

lose nothing, but should raise it up again at the last day." **John 6:39 (KJV)**

<u>To Give Believers Everlasting Life</u>
*"And this is the **will** of him that sent me, that every one which seeth the Son, and believeth on him, may have everlasting life: and I **will** raise him up at the last day."* **John 6:40 (KJV)**

<u>To Love Us And Dwell With Us</u>
*"Jesus answered and said unto him, If a man love me, he will keep my words: and my Father **will** love him, and we **will** come unto him, and make our abode with him."* **John 14:23 (KJV)**

<u>To Send Us A Comforter</u>
*"But the Comforter, which is the Holy Ghost, whom the Father **will** send in my name, he shall teach you all things, and bring all things to your remembrance, whatsoever I have said unto you."* **John 14:26 (KJV)**

<u>To Pour Out His Spirit Upon All Flesh</u>
*"And it shall come to pass in the last days, saith God, I **will** pour out of my Spirit upon all flesh: and your sons and your daughters shall prophesy, and your young men shall see visions, and your old men shall dream dreams:"*
Acts 2:17 (KJV)

<u>To Renew Our Minds And Be Transformed</u>
"I beseech you therefore, brethren, by the mercies of God, that ye present your bodies a living sacrifice, holy, acceptable unto God, which is your reasonable service. And be not conformed to this world: but be ye transformed

*by the renewing of your mind, that ye may prove
what is that good, and acceptable, and perfect,
will of God."* **Romans 12:1 – 2 (KJV)**

To Provide A Way Of Escape From Temptation

*"There hath no temptation taken you but such
as is common to man: but God is faithful, who
will not suffer you to be tempted above that ye
are able; but **will** with the temptation also make
a way to escape, that ye may be able to bear it."*
I Corinthians 10:13 (KJV)

To Give Gifts Of The Spirit

*"But the manifestation of the Spirit is given to
every man to profit withal.*

*For to one is given by the Spirit the word of
wisdom; to another the word of knowledge by
the same Spirit;*

*To another faith by the same Spirit; to another
the gifts of healing by the same Spirit;*

*To another the working of miracles; to another
prophecy; to another discerning of spirits; to
another divers kinds of tongues; to another the
interpretation of tongues:*

*But all these worketh that one and the selfsame
Spirit, dividing to every man severally as he
will."* **I Corinthians 12:7 – 11 (KJV)**

To Make Us New Creatures In Christ

"Therefore if any man be in Christ, he is a new creature: old things are passed away; behold, all things are become new."
2 Corinthians 5:17 (KJV)

To Be The Temple Of The Living God, To Dwell In Us And To Walk In Us, and

To Be Our God And For Us To Be His People

*"And what agreement hath the temple of God with idols? for ye are the temple of the living God; as God hath said, I **will** dwell in them, and walk in them; and I **will** be their God, and they shall be my people."* **2 Corinthians 6:16 (KJV)**

"What? know ye not that your body is the temple of the Holy Ghost which is in you, which ye have of God, and ye are not your own?"
I Corinthians 6:19 (KJV)

To Have A Separated And Peculiar People, To Receive Us, and To Be A Father To Us

*"Wherefore come out from among them, and be ye separate, saith the Lord, and touch not the unclean thing; and I **will** receive you, And **will** be a Father unto you, and ye shall be my sons and daughters, saith the Lord Almighty."*
2 Corinthians 6:17-18 (KJV)

"But ye are a chosen generation, a royal priesthood, an holy nation, a peculiar people; that ye should shew forth the praises of him who hath called you out of darkness into marvellous light:" **I Peter 2:9 (KJV)**

"And because ye are sons, God hath sent forth the Spirit of his Son into your hearts, crying, Abba, Father." **Galatians 4:6 (KJV)**

To Make Us Sons And Daughters Of God
"But as many as received him, to them gave he power to become the sons of God, even to them that believe on his name:" **John 1:12 (KJV)**

*"And **will** be a Father unto you, and ye shall be my sons and daughters, saith the Lord Almighty."* **2 Corinthians 6:18 (KJV)**

"Behold, what manner of love the Father hath bestowed upon us, that we should be called the sons of God: therefore the world knoweth us not, because it knew him not."
I John 3:1 (KJV)

*"Having predestinated us unto the adoption of children by Jesus Christ to himself, according to the good pleasure of his **will**,"*
Ephesians 1:5 (KJV)

To Deliver Us From This Present Evil World
*"Who gave himself for our sins, that he might deliver us from this present evil world, according to the **will of God and our Father**:"*
Galatians 1:4 (KJV)

To Give Us An Inheritance
*"Having made known unto us the mystery of his **will**, according to his good pleasure which he hath purposed in himself:*

That in the dispensation of the fulness of times he might gather together in one all things in Christ, both which are in heaven, and which are on earth; even in him:

*In whom also we have obtained an inheritance, being predestinated according to the purpose of him who worketh all things after the counsel of his own **will**:*

That we should be to the praise of his glory, who first trusted in Christ."
Ephesians 1: 9 – 12 (KJV)

"And for this cause he is the mediator of the new testament, that by means of death, for the redemption of the transgressions that were under the first testament, they which are called might receive the promise of eternal inheritance." **Hebrews 9:15 (KJV)**

"Blessed be the God and Father of our Lord Jesus Christ, which according to his abundant mercy hath begotten us again unto a lively hope by the resurrection of Jesus Christ from the dead,

To an inheritance incorruptible, and undefiled, and that fadeth not away, reserved in heaven for you,

Who are kept by the power of God through faith unto salvation ready to be revealed in the last time." **I Peter 1:3 – 5 (KJV)**

To Make Us "To Be To The Praise Of His Glory"

"That we should be to the praise of his glory, who first trusted in Christ."
Ephesians 1:12 (KJV)

To Be Filled With His Spirit

*"Wherefore be ye not unwise, but understanding what the **will of the Lord is**.*

And be not drunk with wine, wherein is excess; but be filled with the Spirit;

Speaking to yourselves in psalms and hymns and spiritual songs, singing and making melody in your heart to the Lord;

Giving thanks always for all things unto God and the Father in the name of our Lord Jesus Christ;

Submitting yourselves one to another in the fear of God." **Ephesians 5:17 – 21 (KJV)**

To Have Wisdom And Spiritual Understanding

*"For this cause we also, since the day we heard it, do not cease to pray for you, and to desire that ye might be filled with the knowledge of his **will** in all wisdom and spiritual understanding;"*
Colossians 1:9 (KJV)

To Be Redeemed, Reconciled, And Strengthened

"That ye might walk worthy of the Lord unto all pleasing, being fruitful in every good work, and increasing in the knowledge of God;

Strengthened with all might, according to his glorious power, unto all patience and longsuffering with joyfulness;

Giving thanks unto the Father, which hath made us meet to be partakers of the inheritance of the saints in light:

Who hath delivered us from the power of darkness, and hath translated us into the kingdom of his dear Son:

In whom we have redemption through his blood, even the forgiveness of sins:

Who is the image of the invisible God, the firstborn of every creature:

For by him were all things created, that are in heaven, and that are in earth, visible and invisible, whether they be thrones, or dominions, or principalities, or powers: all things were created by him, and for him:

And he is before all things, and by him all things consist.

And he is the head of the body, the church: who is the beginning, the firstborn from the dead;

• • •

that in all things he might have the preeminence.

*For **it pleased** the Father that in him should all fulness dwell;*

And, having made peace through the blood of his cross, by him to reconcile all things unto himself; by him, I say, whether they be things in earth, or things in heaven.

And you, that were sometime alienated and enemies in your mind by wicked works, yet now hath he reconciled

In the body of his flesh through death, to present you holy and unblameable and unreproveable in his sight:

If ye continue in the faith grounded and settled, and be not moved away from the hope of the gospel, which ye have heard, and which was preached to every creature which is under heaven; whereof I Paul am made a minister;"
Colossians 1:10 – 23 (KJV)

To Be Sanctified And Holy
*"For this is the **will of God**, even your sanctification, that ye should abstain from fornication:*

That every one of you should know how to possess his vessel in sanctification and honour;

Not in the lust of concupiscence, even as the Gentiles which know not God:

That no man go beyond and defraud his brother in any matter: because that the Lord is the avenger of all such, as we also have forewarned you and testified.

For God hath not called us unto uncleanness, but unto holiness."
I Thessalonians 4:3 – 7 (KJV)

For Us To "Give Thanks In Everything"
*"In every thing give thanks: for this is the **will of God** in Christ Jesus concerning you."*
I Thessalonians 5:18 (KJV)

To Be Saved And To Know The Truth
"I exhort therefore, that, first of all, supplications, prayers, intercessions, and giving of thanks, be made for all men;

For kings, and for all that are in authority; that we may lead a quiet and peaceable life in all godliness and honesty.

For this is good and acceptable in the sight of God our Saviour;

*Who **will** have all men to be saved, and to come unto the knowledge of the truth.*

For there is one God, and one mediator between God and men, the man Christ Jesus;

Who gave himself a ransom for all, to be testified in due time." **I Timothy 2:1 – 6 (KJV)**

To Remember Our Sins No More
"For I will be merciful to their unrighteousness, and their sins and their iniquities will I remember no more." **Hebrews 8:12 (KJV)**

"This is the covenant that I will make with them after those days, saith the Lord, I will put my laws into their hearts, and in their minds will I write them;

And their sins and iniquities will I remember no more." **Hebrews 10:16 – 17 (KJV)**

To Be Born Again, "A Kind Of Firstfruits Of His Creatures"
"Of his own will begat he us with the word of truth, that we should be a kind of firstfruits of his creatures." **James 1:18 (KJV)**

To Do Well (Obey Authority Figures)
"Submit yourselves to every ordinance of man for the Lord's sake: whether it be to the king, as supreme;

Or unto governors, as unto them that are sent by him for the punishment of evildoers, and for the praise of them that do well.

For so is the will of God, that with well doing ye may put to silence the ignorance of foolish men:

As free, and not using your liberty for a cloak of maliciousness, but as the servants of God.

Honour all men. Love the brotherhood. Fear
God. Honour the king."
I Peter 2:13 – 17 (KJV)

To Give Us A Crown Of Life
"Fear none of those things which thou shalt
suffer: behold, the devil shall cast some of you
into prison, that ye may be tried; and ye shall
have tribulation ten days; be thou faithful unto
*death, and I **will** give thee a crown of life."*
Revelation 2:10 (KJV)

"Blessed is the man that endureth temptation:
for when he is tried, he shall receive the crown
of life, which the Lord hath promised to them
that love him." **James 1:12 (KJV)**

To Give Us A New Name
"He that hath an ear, let him hear what the
Spirit saith unto the churches; To him that
*overcometh **will** I give to eat of the hidden*
*manna, and **will** give him a white stone, and in*
the stone a new name written, which no man
knoweth saving he that receiveth it."
Revelation 2:17 (KJV)

*"Him that overcometh **will** I make a pillar in the*
temple of my God, and he shall go no more out:
*and I **will** write upon him the name of my God,*
and the name of the city of my God, which is
new Jerusalem, which cometh down out of
*heaven from my God: and I **will** write upon him*
my new name." **Revelation 3:12 (KJV)**

After reading the above Scriptures, we can
see that God is a giving and loving God. His

will for us involves good not evil. Therefore, it is **NOT** God's will for us to suffer the loss of our children. And, by saying so, you reinforce the devil's lie; and, you quite possibly put a stumbling stone in front of your brother or sister to cause them to fall.

Don't Say,
"You Can Have More Children."
Chapter 3

*"Hope deferred maketh the heart sick: but when the
desire cometh, it is a tree of life."*
Proverbs 13:12 (KJV)

*"Let us not therefore judge one another any more: but
judge this rather, that no man put a stumblingblock or an
occasion to fall in his brother's way."*
Romans 14:13 (KJV)

One of the most common sayings that
people are told that have lost a child, just as I
was, is that they can always have more children.
This creates a deferred hope. Hope, by
definition, means an *"...expectation,
confidence....."* **(Blue Letter Bible/ Strongs/
Gesenius' Hebrew-Chaldee Lexicon)** And,
when this expectation does not become a reality,
it is very hurtful.

Unfortunately, many people who have lost a
child may never have another child. I never did.
In fact, some will have multiple miscarriages.
Others, on the other hand, are fortunate enough
to have more children.

However, if a couple is told that they can
always have more children, and they don't; it is
very hurtful. Additionally, at the time the
parents are told this, it is like saying to them that
their child that they lost did not matter.

One of my best friends states how she felt
when told this after her son, Alex, had died.

"Just because I could have another kid, it would never erase Alex. It wouldn't change how I felt. If I had to do it all over again, I wouldn't trade the time I had with him." **Mandy Burkett** *(paraphrased from phone conversation)*

Another grieving parent wrote,
"The one that bothered me the most was 'at least you have another child!'" **Anonymous**

These sayings are grievous to a parent. Each child is an individual in his/her own right and means something.

Before making this comment to a grieving parent, ask yourself these questions. If you have never lost a child and have had multiple children, which child could you do without? Could you honestly replace any one of your children? No, because they are each unique and special.

Therefore, when a person who has lost a child has more children, they will not stop grieving the loss of that one child. The parent may go on being strong for the other children, but inwardly they will continue to grieve for the one not there.

Another reason for not saying a person could have more children is that unless the person stating it is God, how could they know? None of us knows what is down the road for another person. Only God truly knows.

As previously stated, I never did have any more children. Continually, I hoped. For me, this created a deferred hope. Hope given to a grieving parent can create a deferred hope that may never come to pass.

Just as the opening scripture above states, when *"[a hope is deferred, it makes the heart sick.]"* **Proverbs 13:12 (KJV)** For years, I experienced the loss over and over again in my mind as well as guilt and feelings of punishment. I felt as if God were punishing me.

Continuing to feel punished stemmed from someone telling me that I would have more children. Not only did I feel punished for having lost my child, but I began to feel that I was continually being punished by not being allowed to have any more children.

This deferred hope became a stumbling block for me. Now, not only was I angry at God because I thought He took my child; but also, I was angry at God for not giving me any more. It made me feel like I could never live the Christian life right enough for God to bless me. It made me feel that God was just out to get me.

So, in my mind, I had messed up too big for God to forgive me. However, we know that this is not scripturally true. But, this is just an example of how the enemy can take your words and twist them up in a person's heart and mind.

Remember, the devil's ultimate intent is total destruction of the individual. Since I believed that I was being punished severely by God, I became angrier at God. As a result, I turned my back on God for almost sixteen years. This was exactly what Satan wanted! This gave him a wide open door to operate in my life!

Consequently, without going into details, I went from trying to follow Scripture and being obedient to out right sinning anyway I could. Rebellion had entered into my heart. I began to do the exact opposite of everything that I was taught on purpose.

In my twisted up mind, I somehow believed that I was gonna make happen what God would not make happen for me. Since I knew that I would never be able to afford adoption or fertility treatments, I was determined to have a child. Infidelity, as well as many other sinful things, became a part of my life. Consequently, it caused much devastation.

One of the things that occurred was the dissolution of my marriage after seven years. Also, at the same time, the emotional torment was so great that it caused me to repeatedly want to commit suicide. Eventually, I received Jesus' deliverance from this.

However, after the dissolution of my marriage had been finalized, I was left with nothing. Financially, I had no resources left. Satan had succeeded in bankrupting me emotionally, physically, financially, and spiritually. I had never felt so alone in my life.

Yet, I still did not turn to God for many years after that.

Why? I could not reconcile in my heart yet that God was good and loved me, because I believed that He was punishing me by taking my child and not giving me any more. It would be years later before I really realized that it was not God who took my child, but the devil.

And, as for not having any more children that deferred hope had truly made my heart so sick. I never did feel like I would be well again. I had so hoped for children of my own that I repeatedly thought I might be pregnant. This caused me great torment.

Repeatedly, my body would give me signs that I might be, and I would go and get tested. And, repeatedly, it came back negative. Although I had come back to church years later and rededicated my life to Jesus Christ, I still continued to have this deferred hope for more children. And, I still continued to feel punished.

But, this time I felt like I deserved it because I had rebelled against God. And, I still continued to have emotional roller coaster rides. However, the difference is that God cleansed me, brought healing for the pain, returned my joy, and filled me with His Spirit.

Now, I had something more to live for. Following Christ legalistically was gone. Now, I followed him out of love. And, I have the hope of seeing my daughter again one day.

• • •

It was not until years later that I found out it would be difficult for me to physically conceive. It was not until I got copies of my own medical reports and was reading through them that I found out that I had polycystic ovarian disease. A doctor had never told me this. This disease makes it very difficult to get pregnant. Eventually, I reached a point in my life where the hope for having more children has greatly diminished.

The preceding story of this part of my life was difficult to reveal. Primarily, it was included in the book to show just how a few words can change a person's life. I ask that you do not judge me. God has forgiven me. And, His Word cautions in **I Corinthians 10:12 (KJV),** *"Wherefore let him that thinketh he standeth take heed lest he fall."*

Now, in addition to telling someone that they can have more children don't tell them that they are young and healthy. They have plenty of time. This all comes back again to the point that the person stating this is NOT God! They do not know how much time a person is given in this life.

Also, this comment makes it sound like the child who passed away was unimportant. It is a dismissive comment, and it is very hurtful to the parents.

Furthermore, it does not matter how old a person is when they lose a child.

"You do not say you are young you can have another one." **Alma Collins Thomas**

Additionally, regardless of how the child died or the status of the child's development, the loss of the child is still very hurtful. Instead of helping someone cope with the loss, the person making these kinds of comments is just trying to basically tell the grieving parent to get over it.

Another comment to avoid that fits into this category is don't tell the grieving parents that they can always foster or adopt. This is simply not true! The rules for doing such are so restrictive. It seems like many of the parents who have such great love for children and want children cannot afford to foster or adopt. Many more children might have homes today if it wasn't so costly to adopt or the rules so stringent.

Additionally, most average parents don't even meet the criteria that agencies expect. My previous mental history might disqualify me which basically stemmed from losing a child in the first place.

Today, I am fine without any medication. That part has healed. My mental diagnosis was not so severe that I could not have raised a child. In fact, I did raise my second husband's grandson for seven years.

However, after seven years, God had let me know it was time for him to go back to his mother and establish a relationship with his sisters. That was like losing a child all over again. If it had not been for the prayers and support of the church, I would not have continued to lean on God.

Likewise, with fostering, the child is always susceptible to being returned to the natural parents. Whenever this occurs, it is like losing a child all over again.

So, to tell a person that they could always foster or adopt a child is not the case. It creates a false hope for many individuals who would gladly do so, but they are unable to due to cost or stringent rules.

And, even if they are able to foster, the hope of being able to continue to keep and raise that child could be dashed at any moment.

Furthermore, fostering or adopting a child could never replace the child that was lost. Even if one is able to foster or adopt, the parent will still grieve the loss of their child.

Fostering and adopting, on the other hand, can be wonderful; a child fills your heart and home. And, the child becomes as one of your own. But, there is still a part of many women that wants to physically give birth to a child as well.

In conclusion, hopefully, it can be seen that we need to be very careful when dealing with grieving parents. First, we do not know the future. And secondly, the things that we say may have a detrimental impact upon them that ultimately will bring them more devastation.

Deferred hopes are dangerous to an individual. For years, I pined the loss of my daughter. But, even after that was healed, I continued to pine the loss of future children that I was told I would be able to have. It kept me down emotionally and spiritually.

Instead of seeking God, I believed with all of my heart that He would give me more children. Children had become an idol to me. At times, I did pray for them. I even prayed Hannah's prayer. Faith was not the issue.

I confessed and called out the names of my seven children that I wanted. I wanted five girls named: Hope, Faith, Charity, Grace, and Joy, and two boys: Joshua and Caleb. I even went so far as to buy an antique rocking high chair and a few other things. I honestly believed that I would have more children.

Approaching 50 soon, now I realize that it probably will not happen for me. It is not impossible but improbable. However, the longing is still there, but not as much as it used to be. If I had known years earlier that I could not have any more children, I would not have driven myself so, which cost me emotionally, financially, and spiritually.

Yes, miracles can happen. Do I still believe that God could give me a child? Absolutely! However, looking back, I am glad that I did not have any more children to drag through the mess my life had become for years.

But, I wish that I could have avoided all the pain that came because of that one comment, *"You are young and healthy and have plenty of time to have more children."* This created a deferred hope and caused me much devastation.

Don't Say,
"I Know Exactly How You Feel."
Chapter 4

"Likewise the Spirit also helpeth our infirmities: for we know not what we should pray for as we ought: but the Spirit itself maketh intercession for us with groanings which cannot be uttered." **Romans 8:26 (KJV)**

"He is despised and rejected of men; a man of sorrows, and acquainted with grief: and we hid as it were our faces from him; he was despised, and we esteemed him not. Surely he hath borne our griefs, and carried our sorrows: yet we did esteem him stricken, smitten of God, and afflicted." **Isaiah 53:3 – 4 (KJV)**

Unless you have lost a child, you could never begin to understand how the parent feels. Parents that have lost children go through such a wide range of emotions. It is quite difficult for even parents to put into words how they are feeling. We will cover some of these in **Chapter 30**, called *Feelings Roller Coaster Ride*.

Even though you read the previous chapters, unless you have experienced the loss of a child, you still will not be able to fully understand how a grieving parent feels. Making the above statement will only anger the grief stricken parents. Following is a comment made by one such grieving parent:

" ['I know exactly how you feel.'] From a woman without children. That is the one time I got truly angry. And she was clueless, totally clueless." **Susan B. Mead**

◦ ◦ ◦

85

Understandably, the person saying this kind of statement is just trying to show empathy for the grieving parents. They are basing it upon grief for a lost loved one that they had previously experienced. However, losses we experience are different from each other.

Here is what Tammy's aunt, who had lost a child, was told and how Tammy feels about it.

"[Others told her... ' I know how you feel, I lost my dog: mom: dad: grandparent: friend'....no loss is even similar to the loss of a child.]" **Tammy McDonald, author of Shifted Vision and founder of Shifted Vision Ministries**

Mandy Burkett, another grieving parent, further comments on this hurtful statement.

"Agreeably, it is not similar, not even amongst those who have lost children. For example, I can state that I understand what it is like to lose a child. However, I could not understand the loss of a child that has been abducted and murdered. I could not understand the loss of the child killed in a motor accident." **Mandy Burkett** *(paraphrased from phone conversation)*

Additionally, the loss of the child, regardless of age, is extremely hurtful. However, I could not understand losing a child after seeing them live and breathe and move. My child was stillborn.

This does not mean that I hurt any less; but my pain would be different than someone who got to know their child. In addition to the loss, they now have the memories of being with their child to deal with. Things around them will remind them more often of their child.

Metaphorically speaking, let's say **Soldier A** is stationed in a country during a particular war that is not being bomb shelled. And, another soldier, **Soldier B**, is laying in trenches with bullets zipping overhead, bombs blowing up nearby, and watching their friends die right beside them.

Although they are both in the military during the same war, **Soldier B** would get extremely angry at **Soldier A** if he stated, *"I understand how you feel,"* when talking about their war experiences. The two experiences were not the same.

Likewise, the death of a parent, a sibling, and a child are all different. So, unless you have lost a child, you cannot truly understand how grieving parents feel. But God can! He sent his Son to take stripes for our healing. He is the only one that can bring healing to the grieving parents. He understands the deepest sorrows that we can feel. He carried all our sorrows when He died upon the cross.

Although, we may not understand the loss of one's child, we can still have sympathy for them. It is all right to show sympathy and compassion for the grieving parents. Just don't act like you understand how they feel. Unless you've gone through it, you really can't understand. And, you will only add to the emotional torment that they are feeling.

Don't Say,
"God Only Picks The
Prettiest Flowers."
Chapter 5

"Hear, O my people, and I will speak; O Israel, and I will testify against thee: I am God, even thy God. I will not reprove thee for thy sacrifices or thy burnt offerings, to have been continually before me. I will take no bullock out of thy house, nor he goats out of thy folds.

For every beast of the forest is mine, and the cattle upon a thousand hills. I know all the fowls of the mountains: and the wild beasts of the field are mine. If I were hungry, I would not tell thee: for the world is mine, and the fulness thereof." **Psalm 50:7 – 12 (KJV)**

"Thou art worthy, O Lord, to receive glory and honour and power: for thou hast created all things, and for thy pleasure they are and were created."
Revelation 4:11 (KJV)

God is an omnipotent God. He created this entire universe just by speaking it into existence. God does not have need of anything. It is we who have need of Him and must depend upon Him. It is not the other way around.

God could speak the prettiest flowers that he wanted into existence. Therefore, telling a grieving parent that *"God only picks the prettiest flowers"*- **Anonymous-** is like saying that God had need of the child. Furthermore, this suggests that children who continue to live are not as valuable to God, because He did not choose them.

Additionally, in Revelation, it also states that God created things for His pleasure. Why would He want to damage His creation? If he were to pluck up a child out from this earth like one who picks flowers, He would be damaging His creation. In the natural, whenever you pick flowers they eventually die. God's creation brings Him pleasure. Death does not bring God pleasure. In fact, God finds the *"[...death of His saints very precious.]"* **Psalm 116:15 (KJV).**

Precious means not only that something is *["...valuable, but it is also costly....]"* **(Blue Letter Bible/Strongs/ Hebrew Lexicon)** Each one of us is valuable to God. So, when a believer dies, not only are they valuable to God, but their death can also be costly to the work of the kingdom of God.

Remember, Satan's ultimate goal is to try to destroy God's people. Another goal he has is to hinder the work of God. He does not want people coming to Jesus Christ.

For this reason, he will attack the saints of God. His goal is to trip them up and cause them to stop serving God.

Following is a comment from one parent and his statement of how this comment made him feel towards God when it was made.

" *'God only picks the prettiest flowers' only makes one mad at God; he should keep his hands out of my garden."* **Anonymous**

Furthermore, Satan will attack nonbelievers in an attempt to get them to stay away from God.

So, when dealing with a grieving parent, do not make the statement, *"God only picks the prettiest flowers."* **Anonymous.** This puts the blame on God. And, we have already discussed what that can do to an individual emotionally and spiritually.

Don't Say,
"God Took Child To Protect
Him/Her."
Chapter 6

"For the LORD God is a sun and shield: the LORD will give grace and glory: no good thing will he withhold from them that walk uprightly." **Psalm 84:11 (KJV)**

"O house of Aaron, trust in the LORD: he is their help and their shield. Ye that fear the LORD, trust in the LORD: he is their help and their shield. The LORD hath been mindful of us; he will bless us; he will bless the house of Israel; he will bless the house of Aaron. He will bless them that fear the LORD, both small and great.

The LORD shall increase you more and more, you and your children. Ye are blessed of the LORD which made heaven and earth. The heaven, even the heavens, are the LORD'S: but the earth hath he given to the children of men. The dead praise not the LORD, neither any that go down into silence. But we will bless the LORD from this time forth and for evermore. Praise the LORD."
Psalm 115:10 – 18 (KJV)

Sadly, many believe erroneously the statement that God took their children just to protect them. Over and over again in Scripture, we find that children are a reward. In the above passage, those who fear the Lord, God will bless them and their children with increase.

Once again, the saying above lays the blame at God's feet. And, this only makes parents angrier. Some, eventually, will take it as a truth. But for most, this comment will make parents want to run from God instead of to Him.

Following is a comment from **Tammy McDonald** and her feelings about this kind of statement. Chris was her aunt's son.

"One thing said to us was that God had to have taken Chris to protect him from something... Definitely wasn't a 'let's run to Jesus' moment." **Tammy McDonald, author of Shifted Vision and founder of Shifted Vision Ministries**

Additionally, when you really think about it, making this kind of statement is actually quite ludicrous. When do you end someone's life in order to protect them? How is that protecting them?

Although there are very many harmful things in this life, death is final. Yes, there is eternity to consider. But, whatever that person would have faced in this life cannot compare with death.

For instance, cancer is a very grievous disease. Now, most people would rather have as much time with their family as they could.

Truly, no one wants to see someone go through cancer. When you love someone, the last thing you want for them to do is die. You cherish every moment that you have with them.

Therefore, it would not be right – even if we knew that they would face this – to end their life years before. And, then say we did it to *"protect them."* **Tammy McDonald.** Not only would it be morally wrong to do so, it is just simply ludicrous to think so.

Unfortunately, there are some out there who believe this way. It does happen today. It's called euthanasia or doctor assisted suicide.

Granted, Scripture does speak of times when God allowed the children to die. But, it was not to *"protect them."* **Tammy McDonald**. It was done as judgment for sin.

In the following passage, they had quit believing in God as their source. They had turned to sorcery for answers and protection. Therefore, they had opened the door to the enemy to bring destruction upon them. And, this caused them to come out from under the blessing and protection of God.

- **Isaiah 47:8 – 15 (KJV)**

"Therefore hear now this, thou that art given to pleasures, that dwellest carelessly, that sayest in thine heart, I am, and none else beside me; I shall not sit as a widow, neither shall I know the loss of children:

But these two things shall come to thee in a moment in one day, the loss of children, and widowhood: they shall come upon thee in their perfection for the multitude of thy sorceries, and for the great abundance of thine enchantments.

For thou hast trusted in thy wickedness: thou hast said, None seeth me. Thy wisdom and thy knowledge, it hath perverted thee; and thou hast said in thine heart, I am, and none else beside me.

*Therefore **shall evil come upon thee**; thou shalt not know from whence it riseth: and **mischief shall fall upon thee**; thou shalt not be able to put it off: and **desolation shall come upon thee suddenly**, which thou shalt not know.*

Stand now with thine enchantments, and with the multitude of thy sorceries, wherein thou hast laboured from thy youth; if so be thou shalt be able to profit, if so be thou mayest prevail.

Thou art wearied in the multitude of thy counsels. Let now the astrologers, the stargazers, the monthly prognosticators, stand up, and save thee from these things that shall come upon thee.

Behold, they shall be as stubble; the fire shall burn them; they shall not deliver themselves from the power of the flame: there shall not be a coal to warm at, nor fire to sit before it.

Thus shall they be unto thee with whom thou hast laboured, even thy merchants, from thy youth: they shall wander every one to his quarter; none shall save thee."

In the next passage, they had turned their back on God. This opened the door for their enemies. God was going to allow and send the enemies of the land to be victorious over them.

These same enemies would take their children either captive or kill them with a sword.

- **Jeremiah 15:5 – 9 (KJV)**

"For who shall have pity upon thee, O Jerusalem? or who shall bemoan thee? or who shall go aside to ask how thou doest?

Thou hast forsaken me, saith the LORD, thou art gone backward: therefore will I stretch out my hand against thee, and destroy thee; I am weary with repenting.

*And I will fan them with a fan in the gates of the land; I will **bereave them of children**, I will destroy my people, since they return not from their ways.*

*Their widows are increased to me above the sand of the seas: I have brought upon them against the mother of the young men **a spoiler** at noonday: I have caused him to fall upon it suddenly, and terrors upon the city.*

She that hath borne seven languisheth: she hath given up the ghost; her sun is gone down while it was yet day: she hath been ashamed and confounded: and the residue of them will I deliver to the sword before their enemies, saith the LORD."

Now, this is not the case with every child that is lost. I am not saying that people today are losing their children because they sinned. In fact, I had believed that for years for myself.

That caused me much anguish. And, it caused me much fear.

God is a forgiving God if we repent. And, I had repented. It is not in God's will to have to deal with us in this way. He would much rather that we had repented. But, He cannot let sin remain. It must be judged whether in this life or after death.

Does God allow for a child to be taken because of sin? It is a possibility. If you look back at the story of David and Bathsheba when they lost their first child, you will see it was because of sin.

But, this does not mean all parents will lose a child because of sin in their lives!

We are not to be people's judge and jury. Not everyone loses a child even if they have sin in their lives. But, sin does open the door for the enemy to attack. Remember, the devil is the enemy, and his goal is to destroy.

In the following true story, God took what the enemy done and worked it out for her good. We need to allow God to give grieving parents the answers.

God will answer their questions and speak to them as part of the healing process.

"[I wasn't a Christian, or I should say I believed in God and that was about it. My son

*died on July 4th; 3 days after his 21st birthday.
He was a major organ donor.*

*I remember sitting outside looking up at the
sky-- white billowy clouds, and then I could
hear the neighbor yelling and then a smack
sound, then crying. She was doing this to her
little boy.*

*I was crying and sobbing at this point! I
screamed at God 'Why does she get to keep her
son, and I lose my son?'!!!!*

*He answered me, 'Why not? I lost my son....'
I still didn't look for God. I was still on that bar
stool.*

*It was later when I heard God audibly. I was
laying on the couch just starting to doze off, and
I said, 'Why,' under my breath....*

*Then, a voice that was so profound yet
tender, but with authority said, 'YOU HAVE
FORSAKEN ME.'*

*I sat up, looked around, heart racing, and
God finally had my attention. My life has not
been the same!]"* **Sheila Auer-Jetmore**

Once again, most children who die do **Not**
do so as a result of sin in their lives any more
than all people who are sick are that way as a
result of sin in their lives. Most often times, it is
a direct result of the enemy set out to destroy the
individual.

Just as in the story of Job. If you recollect, Satan went to God and asked Him to remove the hedge of protection around Job and his family. He wanted to destroy Job by destroying his children. He wanted to prove that Job would deny God and turn his back on Him.

God knew that Job was righteous, because God only knows what is truly in a person's heart. So, God allowed the devil to test Job. And, God limited what the devil was allowed to do. Notice, it was **NOT** God who did the testing or destroying! God restored all back to Job.

- **Job 1:1 – 12 (KJV)**

"There was a man in the land of Uz, whose name was Job; and that man was perfect and upright, and one that feared God, and eschewed evil.

And there were born unto him seven sons and three daughters.

His substance also was seven thousand sheep, and three thousand camels, and five hundred yoke of oxen, and five hundred she asses, and a very great household; so that this man was the greatest of all the men of the east.

And his sons went and feasted in their houses, every one his day; and sent and called for their three sisters to eat and to drink with them.

And it was so, when the days of their feasting were gone about, that Job sent and sanctified them, and rose up early in the morning, and offered burnt offerings according to the number of them all: for Job said, It may be that my sons have sinned, and cursed God in their hearts. Thus did Job continually.

Now there was a day when the sons of God came to present themselves before the LORD, and Satan came also among them.

And the LORD said unto Satan, Whence comest thou? Then Satan answered the LORD, and said, From going to and fro in the earth, and from walking up and down in it.

And the LORD said unto Satan, Hast thou considered my servant Job, that there is none like him in the earth, a perfect and an upright man, one that feareth God, and escheweth evil?

Then Satan answered the LORD, and said, Doth Job fear God for nought?

Hast not thou made an hedge about him, and about his house, and about all that he hath on every side? thou hast blessed the work of his hands, and his substance is increased in the land.

But put forth thine hand now, and touch all that he hath, and he will curse thee to thy face.

And the LORD said unto Satan, Behold, all that he hath is in thy power; only upon himself put not forth thine hand. So Satan went forth from the presence of the LORD."

As you can see, in Scripture, it is not God's will to take one's children. If He does so, it is only because of judgment of sin after offering a time of repentance. And, repentance did not occur.

Or, the death of the children was a direct result of Satan going into people's lives and trying to destroy them by killing their children. He wants them to turn their back on God.

However, nowhere in Scripture could I find that God took someone's child just because He wanted to or just because He wanted to *"protect the child."* **Tammy McDonald.**

Don't Say, "Let Me Know If You Need Anything."

Chapter 7

"But whoso hath this world's good, and seeth his brother have need, and shutteth up his bowels of compassion from him, how dwelleth the love of God in him?"
I John 3:17 (KJV)

"Give, and it shall be given unto you; good measure, pressed down, and shaken together, and running over, shall men give into your bosom. For with the same measure that ye mete withal it shall be measured to you again." **Luke 6:38 (KJV)**

I often wonder how many people really mean this when they say, *"Let me know if you need anything."* **Faith May.** I'm sure that there are some who truly mean it. However, I feel that too often the statement is overused as much vernacular is today.

Has it become much like the phrase, *"How are you?"* Most people don't really want to know how you are. In other words, they don't want to know all the details. They want to hear the customary response, *"I'm fine."*

So, how many people really mean the above phrase? How many are just saying it to be courteous? In today's world, so many people are far too busy. And, grief is something that is very hard to be around.

Is it possible in the back of their mind that they may be thinking, *"I hope you don't call or*

● ● ●

need anything, because all this makes me very uncomfortable. I really don't know what to do."

On the other hand, I am sure that there are people who really mean it. However, we should not leave it up to the grieving person to ask for a need. I think **Faith May**, a grieving parent, expresses it quite well.

"[When I lost my son... people would say to me ('if there is anything I can do let me know.') I didn't really know what I needed nor did I feel comfortable asking if I did. I think we should just see or discern the need and just do it.]"
Faith May

Now, the best thing to do for someone who's grieving is to think about what would help you the most if you were in their shoes. Then, do it. Everybody reacts to grief differently. Some will get up and clean their house and not stop, while others can hardly move from where they sit.

Following is a true story. **Quitana's** mother lost one of her children. Someone should have been able to discern the need and have helped.

"[I was about eight years old. I had to become an adult almost immediately. My mom had totally zoned out. She went days without eating, bathing, changing clothes, or talking. I was left to take care of myself and my brother who was 6 years old.

I would get up and get both of us dressed for school. We rode the same bus so that made things a bit easier. When we got home mom was sitting in the same seat in the same chair with the same clothes on. I had to find us a snack and make sure our homework was done.

When homework was completed I had to check it and make sure it was put in the right folder. My brother was messy so I had to fuss at him a lot. The only thing I didn't have to do was cook dinner. Her boyfriend did that.

My mom was no longer the same. She had this look as if she were in a totally different galaxy. She was here physically but not mentally.

Two months had gone by before she said anything. I was in the kitchen getting something to drink. I walked by her with my cup in my hand. She was sitting in the same seat, in the same chair, with the same clothes on. She looked at me strangely and asked what day it was. I told her what day it was and finally the light had come on. She said you mean it's been two months. I said yes ma'am. She said, 'I have to do something besides sit here.'

I guess realizing how much time had gone by pulled her out of her rut a little. I know that two months is not enough time to heal from any hurt that deep; however, I was glad that she was at least talking again. As time passed, things kind of returned to normal. I think we had to

heal individually and as a whole.]"
Quitana Bailey, Kingdom Swag Magazine

That is a lot for an eight-year-old to handle. Surely someone within that two-month timeframe saw what was going on and could've helped her.

As Faith May had stated earlier, many times a grieving person doesn't know what to ask for. When a parent loses a child, their minds are all over the place. Too many people expect grieving people to be thinking clearly.

However, when you suffer a loss, especially the loss of a child, it is so hard to comprehend why this has happened. That is one place where many grieving parents' minds are at. Daily routines and needs are not a priority. Most are too busy asking questions and are looking for answers to those questions. And, their feelings take a roller coaster ride.

So, many grieving parents need help. But, either they don't know what they need, aren't comfortable asking, or are unable to ask. For this reason, grieving parents need some time and space to grieve. But also, they need to be checked with from time to time to see what might be needed. Too often, after the funeral is over people are left alone to deal with their grief.

But, when you do check in with them, look around and see if you can discern the need. If not, just be there to listen.

In a later chapter, we will look at some avenues where you can help someone who's grieving. Just don't leave a grieving parent with an open – ended statement of, *"If there's anything you need let me know."* **Faith May.** Instead, let them know that you will come see them later. And, keep your word! And, look for a need and meet it!

Don't Say,
"They Are In A Better Place."
Chapter 8

"Not every one that saith unto me, Lord, Lord, shall enter into the kingdom of heaven; but he that doeth the will of my Father which is in heaven." **Matthew 7:21 (KJV)**

"Take heed that ye despise not one of these little ones; for I say unto you, that in heaven their angels do always behold the face of my Father which is in heaven.

For the Son of man is come to save that which was lost.

How think ye? if a man have an hundred sheep, and one of them be gone astray, doth he not leave the ninety and nine, and goeth into the mountains, and seeketh that which is gone astray?

And if so be that he find it, verily I say unto you, he rejoiceth more of that sheep, than of the ninety and nine which went not astray.

Even so it is not the will of your Father which is in heaven, that one of these little ones should perish."
Matthew 18:10 – 14 (KJV)

For many grieving parents, telling them that their *"child is in a better place"* is a very hurtful statement. **Mandy Burkett and Sheila Auer-Jetmore.** One of my best friends, who lost her infant son, Alex, explains how a parent feels when told this.

"[The child is in a better place (Hmm really?! In my mind, all I could think was there is NO better place for my child to be than with me!)]" **Mandy Burkett**

This will be the mindset of most parents who've lost a child. Undoubtedly, most people who state this are referencing that the child is in Heaven, which is the best place to be.

However, because the child is not with the grieving parent, this is hard for the parent to accept at the time.

Here is another quote from a grieving parent who was told this, and her response. Her son was 21 years of age when he passed.

"[People say, well, they are in a better place & feeling no pain! Who says? I don't know where my son is....All we know is we want them back to wrap our arms around them, to give them a kiss, & feel his whiskers one more time. Now, I'm crying & it's been going on 12 years.]" **Sheila Auer-Jetmore**

Additionally, what a parent thinks about where their child is depends upon the belief of the parents at the time. What do they believe about eternity?

Do babies and young children go to Heaven when they die? It is an age old question that is difficult even for the best of ministers to answer with absolute certainty. Therefore, I am not going to attempt to answer this question. But, I will give my personal thoughts on it. And, that is all it is, my opinion.

Scripture, from what I can see, does not specifically state an answer to this question directly. For myself, God gave me a vision as to where my child was. She was in Heaven. Is this true for all babies? I believe so.

Why? Because I believe God is a just God. And, I also believe that children are more sensitive to the things of the Spirit.

You can see that when Elizabeth was pregnant with John the Baptist. And, she and Mary, who was also pregnant, greeted each other. John the Baptist leapt in the womb. He sensed the Spirit of God.

Additionally, God gives us our spirit. *"The spirit of man is the candle of the LORD, searching all the inward parts of the belly."* **Proverbs 20:27 (KJV)**

So, when we die, it returns to Him. *"We are confident, I say, and willing rather to be absent from the body, and to be present with the Lord."* **2 Corinthians 5:8 (KJV)**

Moreover, He knows us before we are even created in the womb.

"Before I formed thee in the belly I knew thee; and before thou camest forth out of the womb I sanctified thee, and I ordained thee a prophet unto the nations." **Jeremiah 1:5 (KJV).**

He knows our spirit. He knows everything that we would've become.

Also, in the opening passage, I noticed for the first time that it said that *"[the children's angels were always before the Father in Heaven.]"* **Matthew 18:10 (KJV)**. At the end of the passage, Jesus said that *"[it is not the will of the Father that any of these little one should perish.]"* **Matthew 18:14 (KJV)**.

Therefore, I believe that babies, infants, and some young children go to Heaven when they die.

On the other hand, a lot has been mentioned about the age of accountability. What is that age? It is uncertain. Why? Each child matures at their own rate. There are some who receive the Lord as early as age 5. I was told that I came to Jesus at the age of five. However, I did not recollect it. Nor, did I understand the concept of sin until I was a teenager.

Many young children know right from wrong. But, they may not have the spiritual understanding of what sin is in order to repent from it.

Therefore, it is uncertain to me whether the child just needs to know right from wrong or has to understand the concept of sin. And, it is uncertain what the age of accountability is.

The story of the children of Israel, before crossing the Jordan River to obtain their inheritance in the Promised Land, is another example of how God views children. He was going to allow the children to go ahead and receive their inheritance, because they did not know the difference between good and evil.

"Moreover your little ones, which ye said should be a prey, and your children, which in that day had no knowledge between good and evil, they shall go in thither, and unto them will I give it, and they shall possess it."
Deuteronomy 1:39 (KJV)

So, it is my opinion that babies and young children who do not have an understanding of good and evil do go to Heaven. But, children who do have an understanding of good and evil and have rejected Jesus Christ, I do not believe they go to Heaven.

Remember, some people's children, when they pass, are young adults or adults. And, to make the statement that *"they are in a better place,"* may not be comforting to them. **Mandy Burkett and Sheila Auer-Jetmore.**

For some grieving parents, they may be unsure where their child stood spiritually.

Or, they may know that their child has rejected Christ and could not possibly be in Heaven. This statement impounds their grief. Now, not only have they lost a child in the natural, they also will feel a loss for them from the eternal aspect.

Grieving parents, who honestly believe that their child has gone to Heaven to be with Jesus, have a hope of seeing their child again one day.

In fact, this hope may drive the parent to draw closer to the Lord. Why?

One of the things a grieving parent longs the most for is to be where the child is or for the child to be where they are. And, consequently, if the child has gone to Heaven, the parent longs to be with that child again. It is a deep and intense longing.

In fact, personally, this is one of the things that had brought me back to the Lord. Now, not only do I long to see my Lord and Savior and be with Him for all of eternity but also long to be reunited with my child. And, I have suffered being separated from her in this life. I don't want to be separated from her for all of eternity.

One of my greatest memories in this life was my mother and I worshiping God together. And, I long for the day when my child and I can worship God together. What a joyous occasion that will be!

But, it is quite unfortunate for those parents who do not have this hope of being reunited with their children for eternity. Therefore, making a statement about their child being in a better place may deepen the wound. They may not have that assurance. And, now they will feel that they have lost a child twice.

You need to allow them to ask God about where there child is. You need to allow God to answer them. Truly, He is the only one that knows for certain! If they ask, He will answer and answer when the time is right.

Don't Say,
"You Have the Faith To
Get Through This."
Chapter 9

"Now faith is the substance of things hoped for, the evidence of things not seen." **Hebrews 11:1 (KJV)**

"Above all, taking the shield of faith, wherewith ye shall be able to quench all the fiery darts of the wicked."
Ephesians 6:16 (KJV)

Imagine for a moment that you are in a skyscraper. You are up on the top floor talking to a friend who is 2000 miles away. All of a sudden, the earth begins to shake. It is an earthquake of a 9.2 on the Richter scale. It is so strong you can barely stand up.

As you look around you, the outer walls of the building begin to crumble. You begin to fear that the whole building is going to collapse. You holler out to your friend on the phone about what is going on. And your friend tells you, *"You have the faith to get through this!"*
Rhenea Smith

Sound ridiculous? Yes, it does! But, metaphorically, this is how it feels when parents lose a child. Their world has just been rocked, and they begin to feel like their whole world is crumbling around them. And, it does not matter how strong they are in the Lord.

Just like that person on the top floor, they have further to fall.

Similarly, believing parents who are strong in the Lord and have a ministry, they have more to lose if they cannot continue to stand. Therefore, telling them that *"they have the faith to get through this"* is not very helpful.
Rhenea Smith

Now, let's take a brief look at a portion of scripture in **Hebrews 11:1 (KJV)**. First of all, it says *"Now faith...."* I heard it said once in a message that it is *"...faith for the here and now...."* It is not for the past but for the present. As previously stated, when parents lose a child their faith in the present is quite shaken.

Next, the verse says, ***"... is the substance of things hoped for, the evidence of things not seen." (Hebrews 11:1, KJV)***. One thing that expectant parents usually have is a lot of hope. We often use the term *"expectant"* when referring to parents that are going to have a child. That term alone means that you are hoping for something.

Also, **Hebrews 11:1** states that ***"...faith is the substance of things hoped for...." (KJV)***. Substance means something that you can actually touch, see, hear, or taste. The verse goes on to say that ***"... faith is ... the evidence of things not seen." (Hebrews 11:1, KJV)***

When parents lose a child, they do not have the living child. When in the womb, the child is unseen. At which point, parents usually have faith that they will be holding a living breathing child. When that child dies, as it did for me before birth, my hope was dashed. And, my faith was weakened.

Faith is like a pregnant woman. She believes a child is within her, and she will be able to hold that child. She will be able to love that child and feed that child. So, she will act on that belief; and, she will begin to prepare because she has faith. However, when that child dies, her faith has been weakened. What she had hoped for so strongly and prepared for will not come to pass.

And, it does not matter whether the death of the child occurs while still in the womb or if it is later on down the road. Parents have hopes for their children. Maybe, it is to see them go to college or have a family of their own. All these hopes are lost and unrealized when parents lose a child. So, their faith can be weakened.

Therefore, regardless of how strong one is in the Lord, it should not be assumed that grieving parents will tap into the faith needed to stand and get through this. Undoubtedly, Christian parents are given the measure of faith needed, but when that faith is shaken, can they still stand? They need prayer to stand while they go through this. They have just received a very destructive blow from the enemy.

Additionally, let's go back to the previous scenario of the earthquake. Now, all of this is going on. Let's add in flaming darts being discharged at you on the top floor of the skyscraper.

When parents lose a child, not only are their worlds rocked, but also they have an onslaught of fiery darts from the enemy mentally. *"What could they have done differently?" "Why did God do this?"* (Even though God is not the one who did it.)

Most of the fiery darts will be aimed at blaming God or blaming oneself. As a result, this can weaken one's faith to stand.

As you can see, in **Ephesians Chapter 6**, one has to pick up the shield of faith when the fiery darts come in order to quench them. Parents who lose a child may be too weakened to pick up the shield for themselves. Others may be trying to pick it up; but, because of the shaking, they just can't quite get a hold of it. This is where your prayers and support are needed!

A good Christian pastor friend of mine shares her experience with such a comment. She goes on to give some advice.

"[When my daughter was born stillborn, I had people say to me things like: 'We know you have the faith to get thru this', or 'You can always try again,' and so forth. I even felt like some of my family didn't care what I had went thru, because they didn't talk about her. They acted like she never existed!

I understand that people don't really know what to say or do during a difficult time like this; but, sometimes it's better just to hold the hand or give a hug because the pain is so great to bear! I don't care if you lose a baby at day 1 or after they are born; you still bear the pain and loss. It's like your heart is torn out of your body!

My advice is be there for the person, talk about their child, and let them talk about him/her. It was a reality! There's not a day that goes by that I don't think about my precious daughter, Christie Leann! I miss her and still love her deeply!]" **Rhenea Smith**

So, please do not tell Christian parents that are grieving the loss of a child that *"they have the faith to get through this."*
Rhenea Smith. Whether they do or not, they need your prayers to stand.

Also, as **Rhenea Smith** stated above, it really makes parents feel like *"[...you don't care what they're going through....]"* This will compound their grief and loneliness.

Don't Say,
"God Ended Suffering
& Took Child Home."
Chapter 10

"Remember them that are in bonds, as bound with them; and them which suffer adversity, as being yourselves also in the body." **Hebrews 13:3 (KJV)**

"And whether one member suffer, all the members suffer with it; or one member be honoured, all the members rejoice with it." **I Corinthians 12:26 (KJV)**

While there may be some parents that accept the above statement in order to cope, for many parents this comment will only make them angrier. Why? For the simple fact, in their minds, the child's home is with them.

Furthermore, now they are suffering, most likely in a different way. It is a deep emotional hurt. So, why would God end one's suffering thereby causing another to suffer such heartache? He wouldn't.

Repeatedly in Scripture, you will find that God would raise up a deceased child or heal that child and return them to their parents. That is how He ended both the child's and parent's suffering.

So, let's look at some reasons why this comment should not be used. First of all, when sin entered into the world, suffering also entered in. It is a part of everyday life. Everyone will experience suffering.

And, what about the parents' suffering? Are they not suffering because they lost their child? Since *"...God is no respecter of persons:"* **(Acts 10:34, KJV)**, why does God not take them home to end their suffering? It would only be a logical conclusion.

Furthermore, in the opening verses, it states that we will suffer as believers. And, if one suffers, we all suffer. So, if God did it just to end the child's suffering, and He is *"...no respecter of persons:...."***(Acts 10:34, KJV)** it would stand to reason that He would have to take everyone home to end their suffering. No one would be left here on earth.

It is not that God wants us to suffer, but we will. It all comes because of the fall of mankind in the Garden of Eden.

Secondly, the comment that *"God ended suffering and took the child home"* should not be used because it puts the blame upon God. **Mandy Burkett**.

Although babies and many young children are with God when they die, we need to keep in mind who is the one out *"[...to steal, and to kill, and to destroy:....]"* **John 10:10 (KJV).** It is NOT God!

Metaphorically, this following idea came from a comment that I heard on a movie from someone with a child getting ready to die. I can't remember the name of the movie, but the concept is what helped me.

Let's say someone robbed your house. They took some very precious items that were on loan to you. When the thief is caught, the items are returned to the original owner. He/she will receive them back. The original owner did not break into your house and take them.

Similarly, our spirit belongs to the Lord. Our children are given to us temporarily as we all will die one day. And, when we die, our spirit returns to the Lord. He receives it. He did not come and snatch it away. God does not relinquish on His gifts that He gives us.

God brings life. After all, He is the one who created us to begin with. It is not a good practice of our faith in God to attribute evil to Him.

When the death of a child occurs, the enemy has rocked the parents' world to shake their faith in God by destroying the child. Also, he will sometimes use others to throw fiery darts to confound them with lies. He does this in order to destroy the parents' faith in God altogether.

If he can get them to blame God, then they may turn away from God. And, if they don't know God, blaming God for something like this may cause them to not want to come to Him.

Below is a comment by one of my best friends, **Mandy Burkett**, on how this statement made her feel.

"[God ended the suffering and took him home. (This helped push me into a rage against GOD and made me run from Christian people.)]" **Mandy Burkett**

Lastly, throughout Jesus' ministry, He did not end people's lives to ease their suffering. Instead, He healed, delivered, and raised the dead to end their suffering. And, He was the Son of God and part of the Godhead.

This should show us that the statement, *"He took them home to end their suffering,"* is not a valid statement of God's character. **Mandy Burkett.**

It should not be used. We should not attribute the death or destruction of one's life to God! God is about life!

Don't Say,
"Get Over It And Move On/Are You Over It Yet?"
Chapter 11

"In Rama was there a voice heard, lamentation, and weeping, and great mourning, Rachel weeping for her children, and would not be comforted, because they are not." **Matthew 2:18 (KJV)**

"Can a woman forget her sucking child, that she should not have compassion on the son of her womb? yea, they may forget, yet will I not forget thee."
Isaiah 49:15 (KJV)

One would think that people would have more compassion and understanding for parents when it comes to the death of a child. Following is a quote from an individual concerning the death of her child and how she was treated. For someone to have asked her this, they were truly clueless!

"Someone also asked me a few months after my son was killed, 'so, are you over it yet?'"
Anonymous

Really! She was asked this only after a few months! Losing a child is not like losing your keys or a pet! Even if it was something one got over with, for someone to expect them to be over it in a few months is ludicrous!

Surely, a person who would make this kind of a statement has no idea what it is like to lose a child! So, I will use a couple of analogies to give people who've never lost a child an idea of what it feels like.

First, for some individuals, it is like an inoperable emotional cancer. The grief cannot be soothed or removed. An outsider cannot reach in to heal their grief. Just like with most inoperable cancers, it will take the power of Jesus Christ to heal them!

This emotional cancer will eat at them day in and day out until it consumes them. Therefore, expecting grieving parents to quickly get over the death of their child will not usually occur. For some, it will consume and destroy them.

Secondly, for some individuals, losing a child is like becoming an amputee. Many amputees have reported a "ghostlike" feeling. Oftentimes, they will feel like that the body part that has been severed is still there.

Similarly, parents who have lost a child, especially the mother, cannot so easily forget the connection they had to their child.

From the time that child was in the womb, the mother was physically connected to it. The child became a part of her. They shared everything. If the mother was far enough along, she felt that child move within her. She may experience "ghostlike" symptoms of pregnancy from time to time.

For many other parents, the memories of the child are still attached. They may turn to talk to their child, and suddenly remember that the child is no longer alive. Although their child has been cut off from this life, the parents may still forget for a moment and speak as if the child was still there.

Furthermore, you would not tell an amputee a year or two later, *"are you over it yet?"* **Anonymous.** Just as he/she has to live with the situation the rest of his/her life, the grieving parents have to live with their child being gone from theirs for the rest of their life. It is not something you just get over.

Lastly, losing a child is similar to a staph infection. With a staph infection you usually have the original site of injury. It could be a cut or something internal. An infection develops that is very difficult to heal. And, the infection can eventually permeate the entire body. Also, constantly picking at an external staph infection would make it even more difficult to heal.

The initial onset of a grief wound goes deep into the grieving parents' soul at the time of the death of their child. This grief will turn inwardly and begin to consume their entire being. Everywhere the parents go, they will be reminded of the loss of their child. They will be reminded of what they will miss out on with their child.

It is nearly impossible to watch television, go shopping, go to church, go out to eat, etc.

without seeing a child somewhere; and, quite possibly, seeing one the same age as the child of theirs that died.

This just constantly picks at the wound. Memories are another thing that constantly picks at the wound. This makes it quite difficult for parents to ever heal or heal quickly on their own.

I think my one of my best friends, **Mandy Burkett**, states it quite well how ingrained the hurt is concerning the loss of a child.

"[Don't put a time limit on the grieving process. I would run into family and friends that expected me to be me after the loss of Alex].

And, they would say things to me like, 'It has been 'x' amount of time. Get over it already & move on!'

(In my mind, I would think, 'you don't have to tell me how long it has been! I know how long it has been down to the months, days, minutes, seconds and eventually years since his death! How dare you!')

The day MY son died, a piece of my SOUL died with him; and I have NEVER been able to go back to who I was before this happened.

I think people have unrealistic expectations of things they don't personally understand.

It has been nearly 22 years since Alex died, and at times I still cry.

The wound has healed over; but, it's still a very tender spot.]" **Mandy Burkett**

So, as you can see, losing a child is not something that one would easily get over. For some, they may not know Jesus and never completely heal. It may even end up destroying them.

For others, healing may come gradually, but they will never forget. Losing a child is like losing a part of you. It is not something that you can forget happened. The pain and the memories are still there. It is just that over time many parents do find some healing for the pain. The wound may be scarred over. But, if messed with enough, the pain will return.

Other grieving parents have received complete healing through the Lord Jesus Christ, but they still have the memories. They have been able to move on with their lives.

And, their *"[...mourning has been turned into dancing:...]"* **Psalm 30:11 (KJV).** They have been able to pick up and put on *"... the garment of praise for the spirit of heaviness;..."* **Isaiah 61:3 (KJV).**

Jesus came to heal the brokenhearted. So, it is possible to receive healing!

However, regardless of where a person is at, the parents who've lost a child still likes to talk about their child. That is one part they will never get over with.

And, it needs to be respected. Just as anyone else would talk about someone who has passed on, grieving parents like to do the same. Don't expect them to *"move on or get over it."* **Anonymous**. That is an unrealistic expectation.

Don't
Break the News Insensitively
Chapter 12

*"The words of a man's mouth are as deep waters,
and the wellspring of wisdom as a flowing brook."*
Proverbs 18:4 (KJV)

*"Death and life are in the power of the tongue: and they
that love it shall eat the fruit thereof."*
Proverbs 18:21 (KJV)

Too often, grieving or worried parents of sick children not only have the grief or worry to deal with, but they also have to deal with the insensitivity of others. During these difficult times, people need to be a lot more sensitive about how they do things and by what comes out of their mouths. Following are some true stories of the insensitivity of others used during such a crisis.

❖ Don't Be Curt, Do Be Sensitive

In the first chapter, I was told quite curtly that my baby was dead by the nurse. First of all, the doctor should have been the one to give me the news, not the nurse. Secondly, the way that she did it was quite harmful.

Medical personnel are often taught to distance themselves in order not to become too emotionally attached. However, some sensitivity can be used when dealing with a loss.

Not only had I not known that anything was seriously wrong, but also I was not properly prepared to receive that kind of news.

It would have been far better if the doctor had come in and said something like this.

"Sheila, we performed a stress test. What it does is to check to see if the baby is under stress and needs to be delivered right away to prevent death. However, we could not detect a heartbeat for your child during the test.

Sheila, I am very sorry to have to tell you this, but since there is no heartbeat, it is evident that your child has already passed away. There is nothing we can do to save her at this point. If you have any questions, please feel free to ask. We would like to help you however we can. Once again, I am so sorry for your loss."

This would have been a much softer approach. It would not have negated the sorrow that I would feel, but it would have helped ease the shock of it all.

What the nurse had done made me feel like I was hit with a semi truck. It had put me in so much shock that I was not able to speak or make any decisions. I was raised in a home where if anyone spoke curtly, it usually meant that you had done something very wrong and needed to straighten up.

When the nurse spoke like this, it made me feel like I had done something seriously wrong to cause my baby's death. Some people are very sensitive people and emotionally fragile anyway, and they need to be handled with even more care during a time like this.

Admittedly, this kind of news is hard to give or take regardless of who you are. However, much wisdom and sensitivity should be used in not only the words that come from your mouth but also the tone in which you convey the message.

Unless you have experienced the death of a child yourself, you never will be able to understand what it is like. Please do not add to the hurt by such insensitivity. You could put someone in a state of shock that they may not recover from ever or fully!

❖ **Don't Call, Email, Text, etc To Initially Notify Family Members Of The Death**

One such family received the news of the death of their child through a shocking telephone call. They were totally unaware of the death of their child until the phone rang.

Tammy McDonald, author of *Shifted Vision* and founder of **Shifted Vision Ministries**, stated that her aunt was called at work by the medical examiner's office.

"[My aunt was called at work by the medical examiner's office. 'Ms. Mosier, this is the Harris County medical examiner. I am calling to let you know that your son died this

morning, and we need to know what funeral home you want the body sent to.'

She said, 'This is a sick joke, and it's not funny!'

They replied..., 'No joke ma'am. Your son's dead.']" **Tammy McDonald**

What a horrible way to find out that your child is dead! First of all, the medical examiner should not have told her this. The police should have been dispatched to her to let her know something had happened to her son. They should have taken her to the hospital and gently let her know what happened.

Secondly, the medical examiner of all people should have known that such a shock could have been detrimental to her physically. Not everyone could sustain a shock like that! If something had happened to her then he would have been responsible.

For this reason, I have stipulated in my final wishes that my dad be told the news first. My mother would not be able to endure such a shock. It most probably would kill her. People need to be more sensitive not only in what they say but to whom and how they deliver the news.

❖ Pastors, Counselors, and Other Mourners—Make Sure The Family Knows About The Death Of The Child Before Trying To Console Them

It is quite shocking when your child dies, but even more so when someone else knows about it before you do. Make certain that the parents are aware before you try to comfort them.

Here is one lady's story who wishes to remain anonymous.

"[My son was hit by a drunk driver. We were at the hospital waiting to see how he was.

I was in the chapel and some counselor came into the room saying, 'Oh Mrs. xxx, I am so sorry about your loss!'

The same thing happened to my husband who was out of town and had stopped at a phone booth to call the hospital to see how he was.

Someone said the same thing to him on the phone. My other son was with him. They just stood there in this phone booth in the middle of the night in the middle of nowhere between Phoenix and Las Vegas crying! It was so cruel. This was in 1990. I am hopeful things have changed by now.]" **Anonymous**

Not only was this a cruel way of finding out, but notice that the woman did not even have her husband with her to lean upon. People need to use a lot more wisdom in dealing with others concerning the loss of a child.

If both parents are living, both parents should be told together so that they can lean upon each other if possible. They both are experiencing the loss. It is something horrible to have to go through alone. So, if you find out about the loss of the child, make certain that the parents have been told before attempting to console them. And, if not, make sure that they have some family with them when they are told.

Hopefully, if you should ever encounter grieving parents or worried parents about a sick, injured, or missing child, you will use a lot more wisdom and sensitivity. Although grieving parents don't expect you to know or understand how they feel, they do desire compassion mixed with wisdom.

Don't Give Despairing News
Falsely or Inaccurately
Chapter 13

"A faithful witness will not lie: but a false witness will utter lies." **Proverbs 14:5 (KJV)**

"Lie not one to another, seeing that ye have put off the old man with his deeds;" **Colossians 3:9 (KJV)**

Dealing with a sick child and facing the potential death of that child is difficult enough. To tell the worried parents that their child is going to die sooner than they actually will can create a constant dread or fear that the parents have to deal with. Doctors are not God!

Following are a couple of stories where grieving parents had to deal with an inaccurate time frame given. Just imagine them wondering as each day passed the allotted time given, if this was going to be the day that their child died.

"[My son passed away when he was 18. When my son was 13, he went into the hospital with a heart problem. The doctor said that he wouldn't ever leave the hospital. After eight weeks of being in the hospital, he got out of the hospital. And he went on to learn to drive and graduated high school. On February 13, 2009, he went home to be with the Lord.]"
Alma Collins Thomas

Here is another example of a true story of inaccurate news given to a parent about the length of time their child had left.

"[The surgeon came out and said Kara had four to six months to live. After I fell to my knees at the shock, I told him he wasn't God; and, he didn't know how long she had. He said 'it would be crueler to give false hope; that there was a 100% chance she'd be dead in six months.' She lived thirteen months after that.

My daughter Kara was 27 when she died from cervical cancer 7 years ago. She fought the bravest battle I've ever seen. When she was given the death sentence, she was already scheduled to be the matron of honor at her best friend's wedding the following August (13 months away.).

She promised her friend she would still be there. She kept that promise although she died one week afterwards. She also walked up until the day she died, even though those same doctors had said back in October 'she'd never walk again because of congestive heart failure!']" **Teresa Pollard**

In addition to inaccurate time frames given are inaccurate diagnoses. These are a form of false hope sometimes given to parents while the child is still sick or injured.

In previous chapters, we already covered some things about false hope. We learned that false hope can be very detrimental to a person emotionally. Previously, the following statements that were covered that can create a false hope were:

● ● ●

- **Don't say that you can have more children**

- **Don't say that they are young and healthy and have plenty of time, and**

- **Don't say that they can always foster or adopt**

So, we will not cover these again. But, this other form of false hope sometimes given to parents arises when an inaccurate diagnosis has attached to it the prognosis of getting better.

Additionally, to keep giving worried parents inaccurate diagnoses creates further hardship and emotional turmoil. They are expecting that the child will get better which is not the case, and their hopes are shattered when they find out the truth. Following is one such story.

> *"[... Dr. Hussein was convinced that Candace had some type of tape worm, and that her weight loss could be explained and easily remedied by this protocol. He was sure the feeding tube would be removed once we jump-started her metabolism again.... While not a degreed nurse, I was more prepared than most to understand the medical terminology.*
>
> *However, nothing prepared me for the psychological trauma. I was on the couch in Candace's room, where the nurse found me when she*

entered. It was roughly 9:30 P.M., and she asked if I would be here at 11 P.M. As I write this sentence, years later, it still causes a chill to run up my spine.

Struggling to sit up, I answered, 'Yes, I'll be right here until we go home.' She explained that Dr. Kundo, a neurologist, wanted to speak to me. I thought, 'Why tonight? I am so tired.' But I told her I would be ready.

Fear gripped me. I was not sure what I was afraid of; I could not imagine what could be wrong. Besides being tired, I was also angry.... Then I heard the words every mother dreads: 'It's not good.'... The doctor explained his diagnosis; he believed Candace had a rare, terminal brain disease called leukodystrophy....]" **Fileccia / More Than a Memory / 41-44**

"*[Rusty had attended LSU Medical Center in Shreveport. He called one of his old professors, Dr. Kiel, who agreed to see Candace. It was during Dr. Keil's examination that our next journey—with a new diagnosis— would begin. Heart failure is typically* **not** *a symptom of leukodystrophy. Over the last couple of months, Candace's symptoms had*

• • •

taken on a completely different life.
No one could explain it; her
symptoms did not fit the medical
diagnosis....

Our answer came from Dr. Kiel....
Dr. Kiel was familiar with the
symptoms of this particular disease.
He told us Candace had all the
symptoms of Batten disease.
We were shocked. We had lived with
the diagnosis of leukodystrophy for
so long.... With this freshness, we
were excited! Maybe there was hope
after all; there was a new path to
explore!...

I was praying for a miracle in Little
Rock, but it didn't turn out that way.
The diagnosis left me upset and
defeated. Even a glimmer of hope
would have been welcomed.
However, I was thankful to finally
have a clear answer, and I was
hopeful that Candace would receive
the care she needed to make her
comfortable.]" **Fileccia / More**
Than a Memory / 67-69

Sometimes, doctors or even family members
want to skirt the truth about a child who is
dying. When they do, all it does is two things:

First, it creates a false hope that their child
will be getting better and going home soon.

• • •

One such thing happened to **Sheila Auer-Jetmore**. Here's what she had to say.

"[First Doctor came into quiet room, and said, 'he was stabilized and breathing on his own'. Half an hour later a doctor came in and said, 'absolutely false--that he was on a respirator and they didn't have any hope for him to make it'......devastation. So I think that was a false hope.

I lost my son 3 days after his 21st birthday. They declared him brain dead July 4, 2003. He was racing his crotch rocket with no helmet for 50.

I had just got home from friends and very intoxicated when a friend of Andrews called me. And, we took off to the sight of crash. I held his foot; he was in back of EMS. They had a bag on his face.

That day at trauma center, we discovered he was going to have a little boy. Andrew was a major organ donor.

I never had Christ in my life. That happened 4 years later. I would suggest everyone to get right with God. Life is so much easier with Him than without. We are friends with two recipients.]" **Sheila Auer-Jetmore**

Once again, medical staff is not God. They can only give a prognosis based upon the information that they have. But, before they do give parents any information, they need to make

• • •

sure and get their stories straight. Furthermore, they need to make sure they have correct information to give to the parents.

If there are two doctors treating the child, who differ in their opinions, they should come together to tell the parents their differing opinions. In one of the above true stories, one doctor told his opinion which was contrary to what the second doctor had stated. The first doctor's opinion or misinformation was given to the parents in such a way that it gave them a false hope.

Grieving or worried parents experience enough of an emotional roller coaster ride that they don't need false hope added to it.

Secondly, skirting the truth about a child dying can deny parents critical time with their child.

For instance, if you tell a parent that they are stable as above, what if she decided to take a break for a moment and had someone else sit with the child and went home for a spell or to the cafeteria for a cup of coffee? What if the child had died while she was gone? She would have missed out on the precious little time that she had left with her child.

Truly, we as Christians believe that God can heal and raise the dead even. However, this does not always occur. Parents love their children, and if their child is dying, they want to spend as much time as possible with them. Don't deny them that by being dishonest, inaccurate, or unprofessional. They will need closure. They need to be able to say goodbye.

But one word of caution! When you do tell them the truth, please do it with great sensitivity. Don't whitewash the truth. For then, you not only are creating a false hope, but also adding being lied to on top of grieving the death of a child. And, no one likes being lied to!

Don't Go Through Child's Things
Chapter 14

"Wherefore seeing we also are compassed about with so great a cloud of witnesses, let us lay aside every weight, and the sin which doth so easily beset us, and let us run with patience the race that is set before us,

Looking unto Jesus the author and finisher of our faith; who for the joy that was set before him endured the cross, despising the shame, and is set down at the right hand of the throne of God." **Hebrews 12:1 – 2 (KJV)**

"Lay not up for yourselves treasures upon earth, where moth and rust doth corrupt, and where thieves break through and steal:

But lay up for yourselves treasures in heaven, where neither moth nor rust doth corrupt, and where thieves do not break through nor steal:" **Matthew 6:19-20 (KJV)**

One of the hardest things for grieving parents to have to do is to go through the child's things and relinquish them. These items of the child are the lasts bits of connection that the parents still have with their child.

It is something that they can still touch and hold onto. For this reason, many grieving parents do not want to give these things away or to have them messed with.

In fact, some parents are so engulfed in grief that they are not able to part with anything of the child's. They will leave the room exactly the way it was. It becomes like a shrine to the child.

Trying to force them to get rid of these things will only compound their grief and anger.

It will cause further emotional damage. The parent must be ready to lay aside this weight for themselves.

Grief is a weight that can beset even the strongest of Christians. And, it is a weight that they have to choose to lay down. You cannot make the choice for them.

Does this mean that they don't continue to grieve? No. It just means that they are not allowing the grief to dominate their lives to the point that it effects their Christian walk. They begin to let go. And, this includes letting go of most of the child's things so that healing can begin.

However, when the parents do decide to relinquish some of the items, you must allow them to choose what to dispose of. And, it is vitally important that when they make this decision to do this, they have your full support. It is a very difficult time for grieving parents. Each one of those items holds significant memories.

Additionally, doing this task alone can be quite overwhelming. I know this all too well. My husband and I had to take apart the nursery by ourselves.

If you do decide to help them, you need to make sure not to touch anything unless you ask first. This shows the parents that you're being supportive while respecting their child's things.

Following is a true story from one of my best friends, **Mandy Burkett**, on how she felt when people messed with her babies things.

"[In my experience, I gave most of Alex's baby things away. I kept a small diaper bag with the clothes he was supposed to wear home from the hospital, a few sleepers my grandmother had bought him and his bottles, booties, hospital bracelet, and baby book (which got left in Michigan.) That one baby bag to me was sacred, and when roommates got into it and used his things it sent me over the edge.]"
Mandy Burkett

So, don't go through the child's things without permission. Doing so is far worse than someone rifling through your wallet or other personal things. The child's things carry such an emotional attachment with them for the parents. If you get into these things of the child or dispose of them, it can cause more emotional harm.

Don't Try To Replace the Child
Chapter 15

"Yea, though I walk through the valley of the shadow of death, I will fear no evil: for thou art with me; thy rod and thy staff they comfort me." **Psalm 23:4 (KJV)**

"Blessed be God, even the Father of our Lord Jesus Christ, the Father of mercies, and the God of all comfort; Who comforteth us in all our tribulation, that we may be able to comfort them which are in any trouble, by the comfort wherewith we ourselves are comforted of God."
2 Corinthians 1:3-4 (KJV)

Initially, people can usually identify with some grief when a parent loses a child; but, the never ending love for that child and the loss of reciprocation of love, they cannot identify with unless they have experienced it for themselves.

After some time, people may attempt to replace the grieving parents' lost love with other things. You cannot replace this type of love. Do not expect the grieving parents to stop loving their deceased child by trying to replace that love with something else.

The parent has to unlock the love they have for their child and begin to share it when they are ready. If you try to replace that love with something else, it can do more harm than good. Such was the case with one of my best friends, **Carol Estes Hare.**

"[When I lost my child at 5 1/2 months pregnant, it was like no one allowed me to grieve. My husband got me a puppy. That puppy

got Parvo, and I tried to nurse it back to health with beef broth and an eye dropper. It died in my arms. I grieved and cried and cried for that puppy. It was like I lost my baby all over again! I wished I had never gotten that puppy!

My word of advice to others is to always allow and encourage those mothers to grieve and talk about it even if they have not delivered their baby! To a mother carrying a child, it is already their precious baby even without seeing it. It is the same way we love Jesus. Even without actually seeing Him, we love Him!]"
Carol Estes Hare.

By giving her a puppy to replace her child, in her mind, it became symbolic of the child. Puppies are very dependent and show lots of affection. However, whatever happened to the puppy, in her mind, happened to her child all over again.

Consequently, when something that is given to grieving parents to make them feel better that is similar but not the same, it can become symbolic of the deceased child. Since it is something that they can physically touch and show love to, it becomes symbolic.

However, when it dies, it is like the child dies all over again. When Carol's husband gave her a puppy to replace that love for her deceased child, which it could never do, it did Carol more harm than good.

Now, Carol has twice lost something or someone she loved. Each type of love was different and special. Even though the puppy was symbolic, the love she had for the puppy is not the same as the one she had for her child. Although, Carol compared the two in her mind when the puppy died, the love for each could not be compared.

Additionally, to give an example of reciprocation of love, let's look at her last comment. **Carol Estes Hare** said that *"[even though we don't see Jesus, we love Him!]"* Alright, that is true. And, our love for Him is different than love for our children or spouse.

However, if Jesus never showed us any love back *(unrequited love)* no matter how much we loved Him, we would grieve. Why? Because we continue to love Him anyway. Unfortunately, and truthfully, it is quite the opposite. Most times Jesus receives unrequited love from us.

Similarly, a grieving parent deeply loves the child they lost, but now they do not get the love in return. They grieve as they continue to love the child anyway.

Thankfully, we have a loving Saviour who loved us first; and, even though He does quite often receive unrequited love from us, He still loves us. Jesus understands how grieving parents feel about unrequited love. We need to point people who have lost a child to Jesus. Only He can fill that void in their lives!

You cannot replace the love for a child or the void of unrequited love in the grieving parents' lives with other things. Instead, you may end up doing irreparable harm if you try to.

Don't Try To Answer Questions
Chapter 16

"In the day of my trouble I will call upon thee: for thou wilt answer me." **Psalm 86:7 (KJV)**

"Call unto me, and I will answer thee, and shew thee great and mighty things, which thou knowest not."
Jeremiah 33:3 (KJV)

Undoubtedly, when parents lose a child, it raises all kinds of questions for them. Questions like:

- *"Why did our child have to die?"*

- *"Why did this have to happen to us?"*

- *"What could we have done differently?"*

- *"Is God punishing us?"*

- *"Why do children have to die?"*

- *"How are we going to get through this?"*

- *"Did the professionals do everything that they could have to save our child?"*

- *"Do children really go to heaven? Will I see him/her again one day?"*

These questions are hard questions. They are difficult for even experienced counselors and professionals to try to answer. Therefore, we should not attempt to answer these types of questions for parents that are grieving.

Furthermore, Scripture tells us that *"[God will answer us in times of trouble.]"*
Psalm 86:7 (KJV)

And, since we are not God, we do not have all of the answers. We need to allow God to answer the questions for them. Truly, only He knows the truth!

For, the answer that we would give them might not be the truth. In fact, the enemy could use us to bring more hurt. He loves to mix a little bit of facts with lies.

And, if we bring more hurt to the parents through our answers, it could cause them to turn away from God. For this, we would be held responsible.

Yes, God does want us to comfort them. And, we can do this by being there for them, praying with them, and listening to them. The main thing you want to avoid during this time of grief is invoking blame upon God in this situation.

Unfortunately, many people will immediately place the blame upon God when they have lost a child, even if they do not verbalize it. The reason for this is that the enemy quickly attempts to sow the lie that it's God's fault.

Consequently, when you start bringing God into the conversation, what you say could become twisted up in their minds and push them further away from God.

Does this mean that we are not to minister to them the Word of God? No, it does not. But, we need to make sure that they are ready to hear it. This is where having spiritual discernment and wisdom is greatly needed.

God can give you a word to speak to them to answer them. But, you need to make sure that you are hearing from God. During this time of grief, these verses could apply.

"But the tongue can no man tame; it is an unruly evil, full of deadly poison."
James 3:8 (KJV)

"There is that speaketh like the piercings of a sword: but the tongue of the wise is health."
Proverbs 12:18 (KJV)

Sadly, if you are just saying what people normally say during a time like this instead of only what God gives you to say, then you could be injecting poison into that grieving parents already hurting heart with your words and not even be aware of it.

However, if you know without a doubt that God gives you a word to speak to them, you should speak it.

Timing is critical. God will give you a word in due season to speak that will bring healing not more hurt. And you can be assured that it will be the truth!

Words carry much more weight than many people realize. During a time of grief, the parents may not always watch the words that they speak; however, those trying to minister to them really need to guard their mouth.

I think one of my best friends, **Mandy Burkett**, sums it up best about trying to answer grieving parents' questions.

"[Don't try to answer the questions grieving parents have. Because the truth is, there are NO answers that can make the loss less painful, no answers to bring that child back.]"
Mandy Burkett

Don't Brag On Your Kids Too Much
Chapter 17

"Boast not thyself of to morrow; for thou knowest not what a day may bring forth." **Proverbs 27:1 (KJV)**

"In God we boast all the day long, and praise thy name for ever. Selah." **Psalm 44:8 (KJV)**

After losing my child, one of the hardest things for me was watching other people's children grow up. I had tried to get over the loss quickly. Shortly after we got back from our trip to Illinois, I went to church one Sunday. I recall that I used to work in the nursery.

So, I decided to go to the nursery and hold other people's newborns. I really felt that this would help me heal. Unfortunately, it did not.

One of the reasons watching other people's kids grow up was hard for me was that I had a family member who was pregnant at the same time. Her child lived. And, I got to watch her grow up into that beautiful, intelligent, loving woman that she is today.

And now, she has had children. Every time I look at her, it makes me wonder what my child would have been like. It reminds me of the stages of life my child would have gone through. It reminds me of what I missed out on.

I love this family member's child that has now grown up very much. In retrospect, I regret what I had said when my child had passed. I was questioning God about it all out loud. I

● ● ●

could not understand why my baby was taken and this family member's lived. We both had done some wrong things.

Why was I being singled out for punishment was really what I was asking? Why couldn't they have both lived was what my heart wanted to say?

But, that is not how it came out. I **never** wanted anything to happen to the other family member's child. And, I did ask for forgiveness for what I had said. But, it still did not ease my pain.

Frequently, I would receive pictures of this family member's children. I would see the love and the fun. I would see how this mother worked very hard to provide for them!

I watched them grow up, graduate, get married, and have children of their own. Each crucial point in their lives reminded me of what I was missing out on with my daughter.

But, it was not only hard because of watching a family member's child grow up, it was also difficult watching other people who had lost children finally being successful in having another child. And, I got to watch them grow up. I went to some of their birthday parties and baby showers.

I was not sad for them. Actually, I was happy for them. But, I desired the same for myself as well. And, it was not happening. This hurt! And, I felt like I was still being punished.

Furthermore, conversations with people became quite difficult for me. Most people had children. And, as most parents do, they like to brag about their children. I really felt left out.

I didn't know what to say. I didn't have any memories of my daughter other than her birth to share. And, it seemed like no one really wanted to talk about a deceased child.

Eventually, I did get to raise a child for seven years. He was my second husband's grandson. I loved him very much. And, I too, finally, had someone to brag on.

However, after seven years, it was time for him to be returned to his biological mother. Once again, I felt like I had been ripped apart. Once again, I had no children to brag on and conversations became awkward.

If you want to understand this concept, then I would like to challenge you if you have children. Just take a week, and try having a conversation without mentioning your children once. Just for a week. It is next to impossible.

It is very difficult. See just how many people that you talk to their children are mostly what they talk about. Then, you will get a brief glimpse of how awkward it is to carry on a conversation for a barren woman or one who has lost a child.

And, if that woman is barren now and has also lost a child, you will begin to really understand the scope of how just everyday life is difficult to live. You cannot go anywhere nor do anything without seeing or hearing about someone else's child. You have very little to converse about from your end, especially if you are trying to avoid gossip. And, unfortunately, I have found that some Christians don't even want to talk about God all day.

Am I saying that you shouldn't talk about your children or brag about them around these individuals? No, I'm not. But I am saying, you need to be sensitive about who you are bragging to as well as when. Sometimes, a grieving parent can handle it, but at other times it can be extremely hurtful for them. Usually, a grieving parent would not think to tell someone this as it could stir up much conflict and friendships could be lost.

They really don't want you to stop bragging about your kids, but they want understanding of how awkward it is for them. I know personally, this awkwardness has caused me great criticism. Many times I have been told that I am not friendly when it really stems from not knowing what to talk about.

Now, it is not quite as difficult for me. I still get a pang once in a while when I see photos of how much fun families are having. And, I still have my days that I grieve for what could have been. But, at the same time, I enjoy seeing others having the good and fun times.

● ● ●

One lady, who wishes to remain anonymous, told me about an individual's feelings on this matter. *"[... after loosing her son to suicide, she asked people to please not send cheery Christmas cards with wonderful descriptions (bragging) about their own children. I agree with that too.]"* **Anonymous**

Receiving these cheery Christmas cards or pictures in the mail of other people's children is very difficult to take. Yet, I put them up on my fridge since I have no children of my own. I show those pictures off with just as much pride as if they were mine. But, I am at a point where I can do this. However, conversations where people brag about their kids are still difficult to take at times.

Therefore, when you're conversing about your children, bring up their child in the conversation. It seems that nobody wants to talk about the person's child if they are deceased. However, many grieving parents do want to talk about their child.

And, if conversing with a barren woman about your children, allow her to be as much of a part of your children's lives as possible. That is one thing that has helped me.

Although it hurts watching other people's kids grow up, it hurts less if I am made to feel part of the family and some child's life. I'm able to do something for a child which is the yearning and desire for most parents.

So, please be careful about how much you are bragging about your children to someone who's lost a child or is barren. I added in the barren woman because it's like losing children you've never had the chance to have. The loss and hurts are there and just as badly. Wisdom and discernment need to be used in this area as well.

12 Things To Say Or Do

Pray, Pray, Pray
Chapter 18

"Praying always with all prayer and supplication in the Spirit, and watching thereunto with all perseverance and supplication for all saints;" **Ephesians 6:18 (KJV)**

"Likewise the Spirit also helpeth our infirmities: for we know not what we should pray for as we ought: but the Spirit itself maketh intercession for us with groanings which cannot be uttered.

And he that searcheth the hearts knoweth what is the mind of the Spirit, because he maketh intercession for the saints according to the will of God." **Romans 8: 26 – 27 (KJV)**

One of the best things you can do to help someone who's lost a child is to pray, pray, and pray. As we read earlier, the devil's tactics are *"... to steal, ... kill, and ... destroy:..."* **John 10:10 (KJV).** The enemy has not only stolen from the parents the child who was a gift from God; but, he also wants to steal their joy, hope, faith, and ministry. His ultimate goal is to destroy the parents. This is why prayer is so important.

Aside from dealing with the grief, the parents may begin to question God as well as their faith in God. Also, depression, hopelessness, and fear can enter in.

Fearful questions may arise. *"What if they had another child?"* *"Would the same thing happen?"* Or, if they have other living children, *"Will something happen to them?"*

• • •

The latter question can cause these parents to become overprotective of the remaining children. Being overprotected can lead the children to rebel against God and family, thereby hurting them and possibly keeping them from entering into what God has for them.

We need to become more aware of the enemy's tactics. It is one of deception. If he can cause a person to turn away from God through his lies, he has succeeded in what he wants to do. That is all the power he has. For this reason, prayer is vitally important.

"Prayers and faith in Almighty God was my catharsis in the greatest challenge that I have faced in my life...."
Patricia (Sistah Pat) Holmes

When parents lose a child, they not only deal with the grief, but they also have to deal with an onslaught of tormenting thoughts which are geared to turn them away from God. Some of these parents know how to stand against the wiles of the devil. But, many do not. It can become too much for one individual to deal with.

If you are not sure how to pray for them and you believe in praying in the Spirit, then pray for them in the Spirit. As we saw in the opening verses, *"[the Spirit ... (1) helps with our infirmities:, ... (2) makes intercession for us, and ... (3) prays according to the will of God.]"*
Romans 8: 26 – 27 (KJV)

Only God truly knows what these parents are dealing with emotionally and spiritually. He knows what is in their hearts. He knows what they need; and, the warfare they are facing.

However you pray, in the Spirit or with understanding, just bathe these grieving parents in prayer. It is most needed!

Keep Visiting the Parents
Chapter 19

"And some days after Paul said unto Barnabas, Let us go again and visit our brethren in every city where we have preached the word of the Lord, and see how they do."
Acts 15:36 (KJV)

"Pure religion and undefiled before God and the Father is this, To visit the fatherless and widows in their affliction, and to keep himself unspotted from the world."
James 1:27 (KJV)

In the above verse in James, the fatherless and the widow may not mean just in the natural. Not long ago, I heard a sermon that really impacted me. I don't remember the speaker's name. I remember that he had stated the fatherless and widows can also mean the lost.

Furthermore, he stated that those who are lost do not have communication with the Heavenly Father as believers do. The only way one has access to the father is through Jesus. And, they are widows in the sense that they are not part of the church whom is the bride Christ.

Therefore, we are to visit these individuals in their affliction. And, undoubtedly, the loss of a child is one of the greatest afflictions a person can experience. Too often, after the funeral is over, many of these parents are left alone to deal with the loss of their child.

As a believer, you may not have all the answers as to why this has happened, but you do have Jesus in your hearts. And, you can allow

• • •

Him to shine through their darkness that they are experiencing.

As previously mentioned, it is not just the loss of the child that is hard on the parents. It is also the tormenting thoughts that come afterwards, sometimes for years. And, just by continuing to visit the grieving parents and being a source of encouragement, you could be the one that makes a difference in those parents' lives.

Only Jesus will be able to heal the pain those grieving parents are experiencing. But, if the parents are not held up in prayer and shown the light of God's love, it could take years before they would even turn to Him for that healing.

Even believing parents, who have suffered the loss of a child, need to have regular visits from fellow believers and to be strengthened in the Lord. As we see in the Acts verse, Paul and Barnabas went back to every city that they had preached at to see how the brethren were doing.

Too often, in today's society, people tend to underestimate the effectiveness of something so simple as a visit. Loneliness runs rampant in the world today because of it. People feel unloved or unappreciated because they have no one to come visit them.

When I lost my child, and the funeral was over, no one came to visit. Eventually, I did backslide. If God's people didn't care anymore than that about what I was going through, then did God care? Weren't they supposed to be His representatives on this earth? Now, feelings of abandonment as well as being punished by God compounded my grief.

However, I honestly believe things would have turned out differently if the church was active in helping to strengthen me through this difficult time. If only there was someone that would have taken the time to visit, pray, listen, and counsel me, I may not have spent 16+ years in a backslidden state.

Although I had spent most of my life in church, I was not aware of how to exercise my authority as a believer over the attacks of the enemy. Therefore, the devil not only stole my child, but he also greatly hindered my destiny.

To this day, for whatever reason, I cherish visits from people.

One of my best friends, **Mandy Burkett**, told me that after she had lost her son, her friends quit coming around. When I asked her about some things that people could do to help a grieving parent, one of her responses was *"Keep coming around and visiting...."* **Mandy Burkett**

For some reason, whether it is technology or the fast-paced day and age it is, the art of visiting people is getting lost. Yes, one would think people would not feel as isolated or abandoned in this age with all of today's technology; however, the touch of the personal visit speaks volumes. Technology cannot replace physical interaction, i.e. a hug, a shoulder to lean on, and hands held together in prayer.

Furthermore, a lot can be lost in a technological encounter. For example, I have experienced many misunderstandings via technology. In part, this is due to someone just being able to see the printed text or email. They are unable to see the facial expressions, hear the actual tone of voice, etc.

People need that one-on-one interaction. They need to know someone cares enough about them to take time to visit with them, especially grieving parents.

Therefore, one of the most needful things you can do for a grieving parent besides praying for them would be to visit them regularly. It matters a lot!

Listen, Listen, Listen
Chapter 20

"Wherefore comfort yourselves together, and edify one another, even as also ye do."
I Thessalonians 5:11 (KJV)

"Now we exhort you, brethren, warn them that are unruly, comfort the feebleminded, support the weak, be patient toward all men." **I Thessalonians 5:14 (KJV)**

In the preceding verses, we are exhorted to comfort each other. One of the greatest ways that we can accomplish this for grieving parents is just by simply listening.

Unfortunately, many people are uncomfortable with this facet of helping others. Death reminds us of our own immortality, so many don't like to discuss it. However, it is crucial for the grieving parents to be able to discuss the loss of their child with someone.

"[Listen to them even if you don't have any advice,]" **Mandy Burkett** says. Too often people don't go to visit or listen to someone who's grieving because they think they have to say something.

However, most grieving people don't want or need you to say anything. They just need you to listen to them. It is one way for them to release the pain, the tormenting thoughts, and maybe even come to the realization of some truth while expressing these thoughts.

Additionally, when one is willing to listen, it shows the grieving parents that someone else cares. They don't feel so alone in dealing with this grief. This can help strengthen them to go on.

However, a word of caution here when listening. A person needs to be aware of the difference between hearing and listening.

Hearing is the actual use of the ears to hear what has been said. Hearing is a passive activity. As long as you got ears you can hear what is said usually unless you are deaf. It may not even take focus or concentration, but you still hear it.

On the other hand, listening is the actual use of the heart to hear more than just the words. Listening is an active endeavor. It takes intense focus on the hearer's part.

A listener not only hears what's verbally spoken, but also hears what is not spoken. A listener is able to read between the lines, able to pick up nonverbal clues, and able to feel sometimes what the other person is feeling.

For example, listening involves hearing the pain, torment, and unspoken things the other individual may not express verbally.

Therefore, a grieving parent really needs someone who will not just hear them but will also listen to them. And, most people can tell when someone is just hearing them or are actually listening to them.

Be a listener for them! By showing them how much you care to actually listen to what they're going through, it will help them in the healing process.

Say Child's Name
Chapter 21

"Listen, O isles, unto me; and hearken, ye people, from far; The LORD hath called me from the womb; from the bowels of my mother hath he made mention of my name."
Isaiah 49:1 (KJV)

"And they said unto her, there is none of thy kindred that is called by this name." **Luke 1:61 (KJV)**

Repeatedly in Scripture, we see that a name is important. It has significance. Often, it portrays the person's personality or character. Also, in the above verses, we can see that God knows our name before we are even born. Our name is important to God.

Additionally, we also see in Scripture that no one can be saved through any other name but Jesus.

"Be it known unto you all, and to all the people of Israel, that by the name of Jesus Christ of Nazareth, whom ye crucified, whom God raised from the dead, even by him doth this man stand here before you whole.

This is the stone which was set at nought of you builders, which is become the head of the corner.

Neither is there salvation in any other: for there is none other name under heaven given among men, whereby we must be saved."
Acts 4:10-12 (KJV)

And, when one becomes a believer, they receive a new name. We already saw that in Scripture when we covered what is the will of God. Therefore, names are very important even to God.

What is in a name? A person's identity, and sometimes character, is in a name. When you think of the person's name, you are able to picture that individual and all of their attributes. They become more real to you and not just a number or object. One should not underestimate the importance of a name.

For grieving parents, many find it hurtful that no one seems to want to mention their child's name. Their child was real! Their child had an identity! And, you can never really truly begin to identify with their loss without identifying with their child. You identify with their child when you speak their child's name. You give validation to that child's previous existence.

One thing many grieving parents would really appreciate is people validating their child's existence and loss through the speaking of their child's name.

"[Say the child's name. Validate that their loss is real; and, their child is NOT forgotten, ashamed of, or an embarrassment.]"
Mandy Burkett

Additionally, speaking a child's name helps a parent to feel that you personally care about their loss. Too often though, people are afraid to mention the child's name for fear of upsetting the parents.

For a long time, it did hurt me to hear even the word **"Joy."** But, it hurt not only because of her death or someone talking about her. It also hurt because, when she died, I felt as if my inner joy was gone as well.

Furthermore, it was hard to escape hearing that word during the Christmas season. It was during this time of year she had died. So, the anniversary of her death made it difficult as well. Now, I desire to talk about my child. And, I can do so without getting so upset.

Likewise, many parents desire for their child's name to be remembered. They want to be assured that their child's life mattered to others as well as to them.

What if the parent did not name the child because it was a miscarriage, or you do not know the name of the child? Ask the parent if they had given the child a name, or ask what they had planned on naming the baby, if they appear receptive to speaking about the loss.

Some parents may have had a name but not told anyone because the loss occurred. By asking if they had a name picked out, this will show that you personally care about their loss. And, it will show that their child's life mattered no matter how long it was.

Talk About the Loss
Chapter 22

"Can a woman forget her sucking child, that she should not have compassion on the son of her womb? yea, they may forget, yet will I not forget thee. Behold, I have graven thee upon the palms of my hands; thy walls are continually before me." **Isaiah 49:15-16 (KJV)**

"By him therefore let us offer the sacrifice of praise to God continually, that is, the fruit of our lips giving thanks to his name. But to do good and to communicate forget not: for with such sacrifices God is well pleased."
Hebrews 13:15-16 (KJV)

Just because the funeral is over, it does not cancel out the memories of the death. As long as one has their memory, the death of a loved one will not be forgotten. Yes, the pain may ease and the healing can come. However, when you truly love someone, you can't forget them.

And, one of the greatest loves is the one that a parent has for their child. Some may forget as Scripture tells us, but most do not. And, if each person is important enough for God to have graven them upon His hands, showing they are not forgotten; then, we should also acknowledge each life to be special. It does not matter if that life ended early or not.

Likewise, for most parents who've lost a child, their child was very special and very important to them. Most parents want to talk about their child and the loss that they incurred. Unfortunately, many people do not like to talk about death and avoid the issue. It makes them uncomfortable.

● ● ●

This has been my experience when trying to talk about my daughter who has passed on. It is like the conversation abruptly ceases. Others have experienced this as well. And, what they need the most is to talk about it.

"[Talk. Talk. Talk about it, and then talk about it some more. (I ended up having a nervous breakdown because I wasn't allowed to talk about Alex.)]" **Mandy Burkett**

In the second set of verses in Hebrews, the Scriptures remind us to not only praise God but to also fellowship with one another. And, that this fellowship can sometimes be a sacrifice. Talking about death may not be an easy subject for you, but it may be a needful thing for another to express in order to heal.

Sometimes, the enemy will continue to oppress the grieving parent mentally. When they are able to talk about their feelings or their thoughts with someone, that person might be able to help them see the truth.

For example, the enemy might be telling them that it's their fault. When they express this, the listener can let them know that it was NOT their fault if that is the case.

Therefore, it is very needful for people to be willing to make the sacrifice of listening. Even though death is not an easy subject to talk about, grieving parents need someone to listen to them. Will you be that someone?

● ● ●

Encourage/Help Them
Chapter 23

"As we have therefore opportunity, let us do good unto all men, especially unto them who are of the household of faith." **Galatians 6:10 (KJV)**

"Therefore to him that knoweth to do good, and doeth it not, to him it is sin." **James 4:17 (KJV)**

One of the hardest tasks that I had to face after the funeral of my child, **Joy**, was to take apart the nursery. Outside of my husband, I had no other help. It would have been greatly appreciated.

Sometimes, when people go through this type of loss, they can end up in a daze. Everyday tasks become quite difficult. As stated in a previous chapter, don't wait or ask how you can help. Mentally, the grieving parent may not be aware of what they need or be able to answer you.

If you see something that needs doing, do it. If the grieving parents have a problem with you doing that, they will tell you so. However, most will just appreciate your help with basic tasks like: doing dishes, doing laundry, picking up kids from school, going grocery shopping, babysitting, or helping another child with homework.

"[Be a source of encouragement/friendship. Help them by taking them out to coffee, going for a walk, or even wash the dishes.]"
Mandy Burkett

● ● ●

For those who know the Scriptures, you may recall that Aaron and Hur held up Moses' hands when the Israelites were battling Amalek.

"But Moses' hands were heavy; and they took a stone, and put it under him, and he sat thereon; and Aaron and Hur stayed up his hands, the one on the one side, and the other on the other side; and his hands were steady until the going down of the sun."
Exodus 17:12 (KJV)

Similarly, grieving parents are in a battle emotionally and spiritually and usually become too weary. Be the one that will help hold up their hands. Support, and encourage them just as **Paula** did for **Nancy** in the following true story.

"[...God knew this would be my journey. He knew I would question Him. He knew I was a strong person— on the outside. He also knew I would need someone super special to walk along beside me. And for this, he provided abundantly.

I have a wonderful friend, my best friend—my 'bestie.' I always ask her forgiveness and say, 'I am so sorry this journey picked you up.' But I am so glad that God picked her to walk this path alongside me.

My friend Paula has been a solid rock through all of the turmoil.... To say I love and value her friendship is an understatement.

She has sat through countless hours in ER waiting rooms, slept many a night on a hospital lounge chair, and has eaten tasteless hospital food more times than any one person should have to bear. And not once has she ever made me feel like I was 'using' her.

The really amazing thing is I have never once had to ask her to 'be there.' I just knew she would be there if I needed her. I can never repay my 'bestie' for what she has given me during this difficult time in my life.

Paula never judged me. She never expected anything in return for her love. On my worst day (and there were many), she never walked away. When the pressure began to build, she never pulled away....]" **Fileccia / More Than a Memory / 61-62**

Don't let them fight this battle alone! You could be the one that God uses that makes all the difference!

Bring a Camera to All Births
Chapter 24

"Whereas ye know not what shall be on the morrow. For what is your life? It is even a vapour, that appeareth for a little time, and then vanisheth away." **James 4:14 (KJV)**

"For I am persuaded, that neither death, nor life, nor angels, nor principalities, nor powers, nor things present, nor things to come,

Nor height, nor depth, nor any other creature, shall be able to separate us from the love of God, which is in Christ Jesus our Lord." **Romans 8:38-39 (KJV)**

After my daughter, **Joy**, had passed away, I got to briefly hold her in the recovery room. How I wish that her picture had been taken then. I wish that some family member or friend had been there with a camera and had taken more photos of her.

Unfortunately, the only photo that I have of my daughter is the one in the opening pages that the hospital took. It was taken hours after I'd held her.

The reason the photo is in black and white is that the color photo shows marked decay with many red splotches. This is the only photo that I have to remember my daughter by.

And, I am not alone in this. Other parents have gone through losing a child and have very few, if any, photos. For this reason, if at all possible, take a camera with you whenever there is a birth. We never know what will happen.

Unfortunately, one of my best friends, **Mandy Burkett**, had such a traumatic experience. Although her son, Alex, had been born, he only got to live for a few days. And, she did not get any photos of her son. This is what she had to say about it.

"[Bring a camera to ALL births. (No one in my family brought a camera, and I have no photos of myself holding my son or any photos left of him. It is all in my mind.) If you are unsure, ASK!]" **Mandy Burkett**

Whether a child lives or dies, parents still want pictures. For a parent who has lost a child, this is the only way they can show off their child to someone else. They cannot physically present the child and say this is my son or daughter. And, they are just as proud of their son or daughter as if they had lived.

And, just as death cannot separate us from the love of God, it cannot separate the love that a parent has for their child. Most people enjoy looking at photos or being able to share them with others. However, many grieving parents lose out on this opportunity because no one thought to take pictures.

This is just another loss that some grieving parents encounter. I would have loved to have had more pictures that I could've framed and put on my wall that said, *"This was my daughter."* I would've loved to have had pictures to share with others.

And, with today's technology, I might have even been able to put the picture in one of those age progression image programs that show how a person would look years later. I would have loved to have tried that. So, if you can, bring a camera to any birth, even if it is a stillbirth.

Give Time to Grieve
Chapter 25

"To every thing there is a season, and a time to every purpose under the heaven:

A time to be born, and a time to die; a time to plant, and a time to pluck up that which is planted;

A time to kill, and a time to heal; a time to break down, and a time to build up;

A time to weep, and a time to laugh; a time to mourn, and a time to dance;" **Ecclesiastes 3:1 – 4 (KJV)**

"Blessed are they that mourn: for they shall be comforted." **Matthew 5:4 (KJV)**

When I lost my daughter, I did not have much time to grieve. Shortly after the funeral, I was taken on the trip to go see family. I think this was done out of love. But, I also think it was done to try to get my mind off of what had just happened.

And, for a time it did. In fact, I don't really recall spending much time grieving the loss of my daughter, other than the initial shock and while at the funeral, until I took apart the nursery. And, that occurred a few weeks later.

Too often, I think people feel it necessary to get a person's mind off of the death of a loved one. And, I think when people weep, some people are scared by that or may even think it unmanly for some men. In fact, my husband, **Randy**, has told me that his ex-father-in-law, as

• • •

well as some others, told him not to weep when his dad passed away.

However, Scripture teaches us that there is a time to mourn. And, that God will comfort those who mourn. We should not deny people their need to grieve the loss of a loved one.

Aside from just stating one should not grieve, or that they need to get over it; one can deny a person the opportunity of grieving by trying to keep the individual busy.

"[When I lost my son, I wasn't given the time to grieve....]" **Faith May**

For most people, grieving is needful in order to heal sooner. When it is put off or not allowed, the grief can eat away at them much like stuffed anger.

And, for the loss of a child, the grief is not confined to just losing the child. Some will also grieve as they remember memories. Others will grieve memories that they will not be allowed to have.

For me, and I'm sure some others, my grief involved never having had any more children. I felt like I had lost more than just my daughter. I lost all the dreams that I had for her, my family, and my life. So, I grieved for over 20 years the loss of my child and any future children.

Therefore, it is vitally important to allow a person to express their grief and not try to get them to ignore it through busyness. And, it is important not to put a time limit on their grief. Scripture says there is a time to mourn, but it does not give a length of time. It will be different for everyone.

Expect the Unexpected
Chapter 26

"The thief cometh not, but for to steal, and to kill, and to destroy: I am come that they might have life, and that they might have it more abundantly." **John 10:10 (KJV)**

"Be sober, be vigilant; because your adversary the devil, as a roaring lion, walketh about, seeking whom he may devour:

Whom resist stedfast in the faith, knowing that the same afflictions are accomplished in your brethren that are in the world.

But the God of all grace, who hath called us unto his eternal glory by Christ Jesus, after that ye have suffered a while, make you perfect, stablish, strengthen, settle you."
I Peter 5:8-10 (KJV)

When dealing with grieving parents, you must be ready for the unexpected. Rational thinking is not always present. Following are some things you might want to be prepared for:

❖ Expect Some Parents to Question God And Allow Them To Do So

Many people, when enduring a loss, especially of a child whose life is cut so short, begin to question God about it. It is a very hard thing to understand and to cope with.

After the initial shock wears off, the parent is trying to make sense of it all. God is very clear in His Word, many times, that if someone wants to know answers or to receive wisdom, they need to ask Him. God is not afraid of their questions.

Here is one such story from a lady who questioned God and got an answer. She wishes to remain anonymous.

"[I asked why. I have heard many times that we shouldn't question God, but I felt comfortable enough with Him to ask, 'Why?!' I felt like He already knew the questions on the inside, so it would be hypocritical and silly of me not to voice them to Him directly. So I did.

To be clear, I lost my first two pregnancies (stillbirth and miscarriage), not a child who had been born alive, but it still hurt. I asked, 'Why?' I asked, 'Why me?' I asked, 'Why now?' (People around me were having healthy babies even though they weren't Christians). Now I understand that God can use my babies even though they weren't born alive.]" **Anonymous**

She makes a valid point. God already knows that we are questioning Him in our hearts. It is really silly not to go ahead and verbalize it. She asked, and God answered.

Too often, parents may be criticized for this. Some may say, *"Who are you to question God?"*

For those who still have children, do not your children come up and ask you questions when they don't understand why something is occurring?

Additionally, when a person is questioning God, at least they are going to Him. If you make them feel ashamed for asking God questions and don't allow time for God to answer them, the parent may just totally turn away from God. This is not a time to attack grieving parents.

"[Don't kick grieving parents while they are down. It doesn't matter if they did everything right or wrong during their pregnancy. The loss of a child still hurts the same.]"
Mandy Burkett

Jesus came to forgive and *"... to heal the brokenhearted, ..."* **Luke 4:18 (KJV)**. Their questions are not going to shock God! He wants to wrap His loving arms around them and comfort them.

For example, during the graveside service, I began to question God. Some of it I spoke out loud. You see, I had a great fear of God already.

Now, with everyone telling me *"It was God's will,"* and *"She's in a better place,"* I felt like God was punishing me. It was if I would not have been a good enough parent, so my daughter was taken away from me.

While questioning God, I was thinking about how I had tried to right my wrongs. I was living right at the time. I had married and gone back to church.

Why did my baby die, and someone I thought had not tried to change, her baby was still living? If the death of the child was based upon how one was living, then why did mine die?

One particular family member, who was also pregnant at the time, became offended by what I had said. She thought that I had wanted her baby to die. That was not what I wanted for anyone's child.

I was questioning that if it was God's will, and He was doing the choosing, then why did He choose someone who was trying to follow Him? What had I done that had been so wrong that it could not be forgiven; and, I had to be punished?

I **NEVER** wanted the other person to lose her child! I would **NEVER** have wished the death of a child upon someone! At the time, I was just still in shock and questioning how something like this could be God's will and why God had chosen me.

Eventually, this not only caused a division with that family member for a time, but it also caused me to turn my back on God. I could not see the justice in it, even more so as I watched on television. People were abusing and killing their kids. I felt singled out with no answers.

Yes, I was judging the other person which was wrong. I have since apologized for my comments, and I explained that I did not want any harm to have come to the other person's child. I was just trying to make sense of my baby's death.

But, condemning me for my comment did not make it any easier for me. Given time, I would have recognized the error of my thinking. Death will come to all at some point and time. It will come to those living right, and those who do not. It will come to the old and the young, because our bodies are mortal.

Why does a child have to die? One answer could be that the child is the easiest prey for the enemy to attack. He seeks *"...to steal, and to kill, and to destroy:...."* **John 10:10 (KJV).**

It is the devil's attempt to get the parents to either turn away from God or never come to God.

The enemy knows many will question God. And, when they do, others will make God out as the culprit, instead of the devil, when trying to answer their questions. This will cause many to run from God instead of to Him.

Furthermore, many believers are aware of the enemy's devices; but, so many more are not. When a person loses a child, it is not the final outcome desired by the enemy. Satan's ultimate deception and desire is to utterly destroy the lives of those that he has taken the child from.

He often begins this by getting the parents to blame God; and, he will often use others trying to comfort them to do the same. Therefore, it is critically important that we don't attribute blame to God for the loss of the child.

❖ Expect Some Parents To Blame God—Even Believers

Whether this happens or not will quite often depend upon the individual's spiritual maturity and closeness in their walk with God.

The devil's goal is to bring parents to a point of devastation where they feel totally hopeless. Hopelessness has often led to suicide.

The losses encountered by grieving parents are, quite often, not only of a physical nature. They can also include other parts of their lives: emotional, financial, spiritual, etc.

As far as the spiritual part is concerned, if a person knows Jesus Christ as Lord and Saviour, the devil's attempt is to get them: to walk away from God, to go back out into sin, and to not receive the abundant life that God has for them while here on this earth.

If an individual does **NOT** know Jesus as Lord and Saviour, then the devil's goal is to get them to never want to come to God. Why?

Losing a child often brings many people to a point of blaming God. When grieving parents blame God, they will not want to seek Him. So, whether a believer or not, when parents lose a child and begin to blame God, they will shrink back from God instead of running to Him. It will keep them from living the abundant life and possibly hinder the destiny God had for their lives.

God's calling on a person's life doesn't change; but, fulfilling God's call on one's life can come after spending many wasted years away from Him because of deep hurt, fear, or loss.

❖ Expect Some Believers To Backslide

Backsliding does not necessarily mean that the parents would dive deep into sin. However, some parents may do this. Backsliding can happen to most anyone. It is quite simply not being where you were with God before. You backed off somewhere. You have taken a step or two backwards instead of closer to Him.

Backsliding can involve:
- ➢ not reading the Word much anymore,
- ➢ not praying much anymore,
- ➢ letting things get a hold on you,
- ➢ keeping you from living the abundant life or victoriously,
- ➢ not attending church regularly, or
- ➢ what most people think it is—diving headlong into sinful activity.

For parents that have lost a child, if they begin to blame God, then drawing closer to Him is harder. It is hard to draw close to someone you are very angry with and feel hurt by.

As for myself, I did try to go back to church shortly after the loss; however, I did not continue going to church. It became too difficult for me. All I would see were the newborn babies or hear their cries.

Before the loss, I used to work in the nursery. When I went back to church, I tried to hold the newborn babies for a while; but, it became harder to bear each time. So, I quit going.

Because I questioned God about trying to live right and still losing her anyway, I began to blame Him. If those living wrong got to keep their children, then maybe I should too. Wrong thinking, I know! But, this is just how the enemy can twist things up in a grieving parent's mind.

I began to question my beliefs. I lost all trust and confidence in God at that point to protect me and mine. So, I left the church and delved headlong into sin.

In fact, I remember, quite sadly, that I went to visit my parents. On Sunday, they expected us to go to church. I was adamant that I was not going to go. They insisted we go. So, my husband and I packed up our bags and headed back home while my parents went on to church.

It was well over 16 years before I could go back to church and give my heart back to God. Sixteen wasted years; and, it was all because I fell for one of the biggest traps of the enemy—

the blame game. It is as old as the Garden of Eden.

Because of my sinfulness, eventually I lost everything including my husband. The enemy not only took my child, but he also tripped me up, tortured my mind, took my husband from me, and took any finances that I had as well. I was bankrupt all the way around.

❖ Expect Some Parents To Have Fits Of Outrage

Some parents will be so grief stricken and angry, and they won't know what to do with that anger. Therefore, the anger just builds and builds until they have an explosive outburst. This could lead to damage to property or even accidentally hurting someone. It could also lead to legal trouble.

These individuals may have even been a typically quiet person. However, other pains and hurts that may not have been previously dealt with and buried could trigger an outrage episode when they lose a child.

Grieving parents should be allowed to express their anger in a healthy manner to help avoid an outrage episode that can lead to further problems.

❖ Expect Some Parents To Go On Shopping Sprees Or Excessively Give Away Things

This was one of my downfalls. And, it caused me quite a bit of financial distress. Eventually, it led to even writing bad checks for a period of time. After returning to God, a pastor spoke truth into my life about this. He let me know that writing a bad check was the same as stealing. Since I did not want to be considered a thief, I quit intentionally writing bad checks.

However, when I did it in the past, it was usually around Christmas time. I didn't want to just buy one gift for my second husband's children and grandchildren. It became an obsession to buy out the stores so to speak. I could easily spend up to $300 per child not to mention other family members.

Eventually, credit instead of bad checks replaced this obsession. If my child had survived, I wanted her to have the best. I never wanted her to lack anything. And, since I could not do that for her, I would do it for others and their children to excess. To this day, I still go a little overboard on gifts for others. I love to give gifts.

While my obsession was shopping, other grieving parents' obsessions may be to give away things. It may begin by giving away the child's things that was lost, but end up being most everything they own.

❖ Expect Some Parents To Cry Uncontrollably

Over the years, I had noticed that it does not take much to make me cry about anything. It could be a photo of someone else's child, a good report of a time that they have had with their child, or just something as simple as seeing baby clothes in the store. One of the biggest things that will make me cry is Mother's Day and baby showers.

And, quite often, I find myself crying over stupid things. I'm sure somewhere it is rooted in something that reminded me of the loss. So, don't be too hard on individuals who seem to be a little sensitive. There just may be a reason for the tears even if they can't tell you why.

❖ Expect Some Parents To Just Want To Sit And Stare At Their Child's Things Or Make The Child's Room A Shrine

Some grieving parents may have a difficulty in letting go. Therefore, they may sit there for hours or days on end just staring at their child's things.

Others may want to keep the child's room exactly the way it was and not allow access to that room. These individuals are having a really tough time with the loss of their child.

And, to let go of these things, they may feel like they are losing their child all over again. They may fear that they will forget their child.

Those items are like a security blanket to them. They may feel if they let them go they would totally fall apart. Don't try to push them into giving those things away. It is hard enough to do it in the first place.

Furthermore, if you try to force it before they are ready, you may cause even further severe emotional trauma. Letting go of the things is not letting go of the memory of the child. However, the parents must realize this for themselves. So, expect some parents to hang on to a few items or keep a whole roomful of the child's belongings.

❖ **Expect That Some Grieving Parents May Attempt To Harm Themselves**

Some people may not realize the tormenting thoughts, agony, and depression, associated with the loss of a child. The pain can become too intolerable.

However, these parents have to continue trying to go on and to live. They have to work, take care of their home and finances, and maybe even other children. Some feel that if they release that pain they will fall apart and not be able to do these things.

Therefore, some grieving parents may turn to harmful things to ease the pain. It could be drugs, alcohol, over eating, under eating, or self-mutilation.

Recently, I have heard and seen more and more about people who are what they call "cutters." They believe that if they feel physical pain, then, they won't feel the emotional pain.

Years ago, I used to be an attempted "cutter." Fear of dying was the only thing that kept me from cutting past the first layer of skin. After I came back to church, the same pastor who told me about the checks also told me that I didn't have to do this anymore. Jesus had delivered me. It was so freeing, and I will never forget the day at the altar when Jesus took my pain away while filling me with His Spirit.

If you know someone who is a "cutter," they really need for you to intercede on their behalf. They need deliverance from this. They are tortured in their minds and cannot find any relief. Jesus is the only one who can bring them this relief.

❖ **Expect Some Parents To Become Forgetful**

As previously expressed, grieving parents have so much going on in their minds. Aside from the grief and sorrow they feel in their hearts, they may be also dealing with other tormenting types of thoughts. Some may become so disconnected and just go through the motions. They may not even remember doing things.

So, when dealing with grieving parents, it is vitally important that someone step up to help remind them of important things such as appointments, taking medications, and maybe even eating. And, if you sent an invitation to grieving parents for something, don't be angry if they don't show. They may have forgotten.

❖ Expect Some Parents To Grow Stronger In The Lord Because Of The Loss

When I first lost my daughter, I attempted to go back to church. I continued to praise the Lord for a time. However, I received little support from my brothers and sisters in the Lord. And, I did not know how to apply *"... the weapons of our warfare...."* **2 Corinthians 10:4 (KJV).** Eventually, I dropped out of church and backslid for many years.

However, I have seen several couples in my life that have lost a child grow stronger in the Lord. I saw them continue to attend church, worship and praise the Lord, and even foster or adopt other children. Some have gone on to tell their stories or invest in other children.

Did these individuals not suffer some of the same irrational or tormenting thoughts? I believe they did, but I believe they knew how to stand. And, they knew who their healer and deliverer was.

The key thing from this chapter is to expect the unexpected when dealing with grieving parents who have lost a child. Many grieving parents have to push through a lot of irrational thoughts.

Self-mutilation and self-harm are irrational thoughts. Some people have the strength to overcome these thoughts. Many don't. Some are Christians, but they are not spiritually strong enough to stand during this battle. They may not know how to apply the principles of spiritual warfare given in the Scriptures.

Often, churches will teach that we have spiritual warfare and need to *"[cast down imaginations,...]"* **2 Corinthians 10:5 (KJV).** And, they teach that we have the tools to defeat the enemy; but, many neglect to teach us how to apply *"... the weapons of our warfare...."* **2 Corinthians 10:4 (KJV).**

If people try to stand in their own strength, they will surely fall. And, if we try to fight a battle with the enemy, that has already been won through Jesus Christ, instead of exercising our authority through Jesus' name and blood, we will fall.

This is where other believers, who understand spiritual warfare, intercession, and deliverance, really need to stand in the gap for these parents.

Encourage Them to Plant Love Seeds
Chapter 27

"Charity never faileth:....And now abideth faith, hope, charity, these three; but the greatest of these is charity."
I Corinthians 13:8a, 13 (KJV)

"They that sow in tears shall reap in joy."
Psalm 126:5 (KJV)

Charity in the above verse is the agape type of love. **(Blue Letter Bible/Strongs/Greek Lexicon)** It is the type of love that Jesus Christ has for us. He knows what it feels like to have unrequited love.

Unrequited just simply means that it is love that is not answered or given back in return. **(Microsoft Word Thesaurus: English U.S.)**

Today, many people still reject Jesus. So, Jesus understands the heart of those aching to give love to their child and to receive that love in return. It is hard pressed to find a love on this earth that is purer than the innocent love that young children have for their parents.

Early on, children want to show their affection and give hugs to their parents or give them a kiss. They don't need a reason other than they just love their parents and want to show it.

Likewise, parents want to show their affection and love to their children no matter what age the children are when they die. When the children die, many parents desire to have that one more hug or one more kiss from their child. They want to hear their child say that they love them too.

Somehow, before the child is even born, most parents have a deep love for that child. They want to give that child this love. For, when you show love to others, it is like a seed. When it is planted and grows, one reaps a harvest. And, that harvest is one of love from their own children.

Unfortunately, those who have lost a child, now have to find a different place to plant that seed. Love is not meant to be held onto with so tight a grip. When one does, it eventually turns inward and becomes soured. It is something that needs to be given to another.

❖ Do Gently Encourage Them To Plant Seeds Of Love

After some time to grieve has been allowed, gradually and gently encourage them to plant seeds of love. This can be done in several ways. It may be done by babysitting other people's kids or letting them take your kids to the park, etc.

It can be done by donating funds to an organization that helps underprivileged children. For example, one woman started the **Tysean Thomas Friends and Family Scholarship Fund** in honor of her son that had passed away.

"[Another step towards my healing, I turned my pain into my purpose; and, I established the

Tysean Thomas Friends and Family Scholarship Fund. Last year, we was able to give a young man a $500 scholarship. And, this year, on April 17, we will have the second annual Tysean Thomas Friends and Family Scholarship fundraiser.

After my son passed away, the funeral expenses were astronomical. And, the one thing that helps me out a lot during this time was the fundraiser for these funeral expenses that my family and coworkers started. All the needed funds were raised. In fact, I had to tell the fundraisers to stop raising more funds.]"
Alma Collins Thomas

Planting seeds of love could be something as simple as buying a gift for a child that is on the angel tree at Christmas time, or it could be collecting toys throughout the year and donating them during the holidays.

Although planting this seed of love on others will never stop the love for their child, it will help in easing the pain some and keep one from getting so bitter inside.

God has shown me so much love from Him and through others because of this principle. It does not make me love my daughter any less, but it has helped ease my pain. Just to give love to a child, and as most children do to show appreciation, they may just come up and give me a hug.

Maybe that child is not receiving love from their parents like they need to. And, you have a lot of love to give.

Although I had very loving parents, I was a middle child. And, I will never forget a couple at church who took me under their wings. I sat with them at church. They gave me gifts sometimes for no reason. It wasn't a holiday or anything. Or, they took me out for a milkshake. It made me feel very special; and, I still love those people today and remember them.

Planting love seeds into another child's life operates under the principles of sowing and reaping. And, like the book of Psalm says in the opening verses, the sowing may be done tearfully.

Yes, as you invest into another child's life, memories of the loss of your own child may bring tears to your eyes. However, Scripture promises that you will reap joy. There's just something about giving that brings such joy to your heart.

Although, you may feel like you have lost everything when you lost a child, you haven't. You still have the ability to give love.

Love is the greatest thing that you can give to another. It can make all the difference in another child's life. By planting a seed of love, you could be making an eternal difference in that child's life. As you plant love seeds, you will receive love in return. And, that love can come from anyone.

When you are giving and receiving love, it is more difficult for bitterness to develop in your heart. Why? Because love is not selfish.

Love focuses on another instead of oneself. However, bitterness focuses on your own hurts, desires, and rights. So, it is very important, even for the grieving parents, to plant seeds of love. It will help aid in the healing process.

Memorialize the Child Somehow
Chapter 28

*"Let not your heart be troubled: ye believe in God,
believe also in me.*

*In my Father's house are many mansions: if it were not
so, I would have told you. I go to prepare a place for you.*

*And if I go and prepare a place for you, I will come
again, and receive you unto myself; that where I am, there
ye may be also."* **John 14:1-3 (KJV)**

*"But Jesus said, Suffer little children, and forbid them
not, to come unto me: for of such is the kingdom of
heaven."* **Matthew 19:14 (KJV)**

One thing that grieving parents really want
to know is that their child will be remembered. I
will never forget how honored I felt when my
parents chose to memorialize my daughter, **Joy**.

For years, my parents contributed to **Feed
the Children** in memory of my daughter. This
brought such great joy to my heart – to know
that her memory would live on and that another
child was being helped.

Another thing one of my family members
did to memorialize my daughter was to make
key chains with her photo on it. Although the
timing was off, I greatly appreciated having
these. Currently, they are stored in my
footlocker with my most cherished things.

There are many ways one can help to memorialize someone's child. There are tons of places that you can donate in the memory of someone. Also, some parents, like Doran and I, could not afford a headstone. If you have the capability to help someone out in getting one for their deceased child, it would be greatly appreciated.

Another way to memorialize the child who has passed away is to write a book. Many grieving parents or family members have already done this. It not only helps them sort through some of their feelings, but it helps the parents to know that their child's name will live on.

Whatever it is you choose to do for the parents to memorialize their child, you may want to ask first. Also, you need to make sure of the timing. Some grieving parents may have a difficulty accepting your gift of love if you do this around the anniversary date of the death of their child.

During this period of time, all the emotions tend to come flooding back. And, it is just not the proper time to approach them with this. This time frame could be anywhere from a month or so around the anniversary date. It's doesn't just include the date of death itself.

However, most grieving parents will truly appreciate your gift of love. It will bring them some joy knowing that someone else cared enough about their loss and wants to remember with them the name of their child. It makes the load a little easier to bear knowing that they are not remembering their child alone.

Remember the Parents on Holidays
Chapter 29

"And let us consider one another to provoke unto love and to good works:

Not forsaking the assembling of ourselves together, as the manner of some is; but exhorting one another: and so much the more, as ye see the day approaching."
Hebrews 10:24-25 (KJV)

"And they continued stedfastly in the apostles' doctrine and fellowship, and in breaking of bread, and in prayers." **Acts 2:42 (KJV)**

Aside from the actual loss of the child and the funeral, the other two hardest times for grieving parents are the anniversary date of the loss and holidays. For some parents, especially those who don't have any other children, the holidays have now become quite lonely.

During the holiday season, people tend to spend time just with their families and forget those who can't be with theirs, or those who don't have any family around nearby. Throw in the loss of a child that might have been there, and this loneliness and depression is compounded for these parents.

One of the hardest holidays for grieving parents is Mother's Day and Father's Day. And, if the grieving parents do go to church, it can become quite confusing.

I found it most difficult on Mother's Day to attend church. I was torn. At church, the mothers were being honored. Children were making gifts for their mothers in class. Churches would give gifts to the mothers.

And, when the time would come for the mothers to take a gift, I would be torn as whether to take one or not. Some people would insist that I did; yet, I did not feel like a mother. My daughter was stillborn. But on the other hand, I do have a child who is in heaven.

Eventually, because of others' insistence, I would take home the gift. I remember on one occasion a mother who had three children had lost her gift; and, she was giving us a ride home. So, I gave her my gift. This duality of feeling like a mother, yet not, is very tormenting.

And, after the services were over, I got to witness other children giving their mothers gifts that they had made in Sunday School. I got to watch while other mothers are taken out to dinner and treated really special. Feelings of loss, rejection, abandonment, and depression just began to overwhelm me.

Now, it is not just the loss of the child I am dealing with. It is the loss of all the love, honor, and time I would have received from my child.

Often times, in most churches, grieving mothers are forgotten about. But I really appreciated what **Joyce Irving**, my Assistant Pastor and one of my best friends, did one Sunday morning on Mother's Day at church. She didn't just mention the mothers with living children. She gave recognition to the mothers who had lost a child.

And, when I knew beforehand that she was going to do this, God gave me the poem that is in this book. It was read that Sunday morning. We were not forgotten that day, and it meant a whole lot.

Another difficult holiday for many grieving parents is Christmas. It is a time that families spend together. And, many parents enjoy buying gifts for their children and watching their delight as they open up their packages. For grieving parents, they do not get to do this for their child. They miss out on this.

Below are a couple of true stories from some women who share their struggles with the holidays because of the loss of a child.

"Holidays are still difficult especially Christmas. Before my daughter gets up of the morning to open up her gifts, I still take time to cry in grief for my son." **Alma Collins Thomas**

"[...My daughter left behind two daughters which I cared for. When the Holidays and my children's birthdays come, it's a very emotional time. I have learned it gets easier with time ... There are certain times that their memory breaks my heart....]" **Shirley Denton**

Additionally, Christmas time is difficult for me, because it is also the anniversary date for the loss of my daughter. I lost her just 12 days before Christmas. And, for a long time, I could not even enjoy the song, *"Joy To The World."*

Why? Because I had named my daughter **Joy**. And, many Christmas songs have that word in it. It was like rubbing salt into an open wound. One of the ways that I dealt with the grief, as mentioned earlier, was shopping and giving to other people's children.

And, it was even more difficult for me during Christmas as I watched other family members' children open gifts. Thinking about it now though, my daughter has the greatest gift possible. She is with Jesus, and she has absolutely everything she could possibly need!

And, I believe she's up there praising Him. Her heart is so full of Joy, and she is probably praising up a storm!

Another holiday that is difficult for some parents is Easter. This is the case for one of my best friends, **Mandy Burkett**. And, I think she put it best concerning all holidays how one feels.

She said, *"It's hard for me because Easter was early that year, and on the day that I lost my son. Here everybody was being so cheery. It was pink and blue bunnies everywhere. How was I supposed to be so cheerful when I had just lost my son?"* **Mandy Burkett** *(paraphrased from phone conversation)*

Whatever holiday it is, grieving parents are really torn. They don't want to bring everybody else down; yet, they are hurting very deeply and are very sad inside.

One of the best ways that you can help them during this time is not to expect them to be cheery. Another way is to somehow recognize how they must be feeling during this time.

Spend some time with them during the holidays. The more time that they spend alone, the deeper and darker it feels for them. They just want somebody to care.

If you have multiple children, maybe let them adopt one of your kids for that holiday. Treat them as part of your family.

Also, holidays are not the only thing that's difficult. Baby showers are too. Don't be insensitive and leave them out. Invite them anyway and let them decide whether they think they can handle going or not.

Don't criticize them if they don't show. If they do show up to the baby shower, don't force them to do anything they don't want to do-- for example, holding the baby. They are doing well just to be there to support you.

It is a very difficult thing for someone to be joyful for someone else when you are experiencing so much hurt and pain yourself. But, by them appearing, they are trying to.

Don't treat them like they are brittle. But, make sure you offer to include them in what's going on. Don't just let them sit in the corner alone.

Give them the opportunity to work through their emotions while participating. It's part of the healing process. Because everywhere they go, they are going to see children and must be able to deal with it.

The main thing to remember here is that during the holidays grieving parents are having a really difficult time. If there is any way that you can include them along with your family or spend time with them, it would be greatly beneficial.

Feelings of loneliness compounded with grief make it extremely difficult for these parents to get through the holidays. Be a part of their lives during this time. Let them know they are not forgotten. Let them know that they are loved.

Feelings Roller Coaster Ride
Chapter 30

"Seeing then that we have a great high priest, that is passed into the heavens, Jesus the Son of God, let us hold fast our profession.

For we have not an high priest which cannot be touched with the feeling of our infirmities; but was in all points tempted like as we are, yet without sin.

Let us therefore come boldly unto the throne of grace, that we may obtain mercy, and find grace to help in time of need." **Hebrews 4:14-16 (KJV)**

"He is despised and rejected of men; a man of sorrows, and acquainted with grief: and we hid as it were our faces from him; he was despised, and we esteemed him not.

Surely he hath borne our griefs, and carried our sorrows: yet we did esteem him stricken, smitten of God, and afflicted.

But he was wounded for our transgressions, he was bruised for our iniquities: the chastisement of our peace was upon him; and with his stripes we are healed."
Isaiah 53:3-5 (KJV)

Unless you have gone through the loss of a child, you can never really truly understand the range of emotions that grieving parents may feel.

"[I lost two adult children....Yes, I would like to share my experience with the emotions with grieving. I wrote two books on grieving. My emotions were like riding a roller coaster. My life was suddenly turned up side down causing anxiety and great loss,....]"
Shirley Denton

● ● ●
229

The loss of a child is such a traumatic event for parents who are grieving that they may cycle through different emotions all in the same day. One minute they could be laughing; and, the next, they could be weeping uncontrollably. For this reason, sometimes the best thing you can do is to just listen.

In this chapter, we will go through some of the emotions that grieving parents may feel at any given moment. These feelings can cause great misunderstandings.

For several years, one of my best friends and I have had a standing joke. She would often tell people *"Sheila is often misunderstood. But, after you get to know her, you will begin to understand her better."* **Anonymous**

And, I recall her saying one time, that in the past, *"she would have rather eaten glass at times than to have spoken with me."* **Anonymous.**

We laugh about this, because she understands me and the emotional roller coaster ride that I've been on since the death of my child. We did not meet for about 8-10 years after the death of my child. So, as you can see, the emotional roller coaster can go on for years.

Also, she used say to people, *"I can tell what mood Sheila is in just by the back of her head when she walks into the church."* **Anonymous**

I'm a very open person with my emotions and very sensitive. And, part of the reason people misunderstand me is a result of the emotional roller coaster ride that I have been on for the past 31 years. Although it has improved some, I still battle with oversensitivity and some of the following emotional states at times.

As you read through the different emotions that I and some others have experienced, sometimes all in one day, you'll begin to understand why grieving parents are sometimes so misunderstood.

And, this is why I'm glad that God understands us and loves us as we are. God has brought some healing in some of these areas to me. And, I believe complete healing will come.

Now, some of these comments may be difficult to read. But, to really understand what a grieving parent might be going through, it would be beneficial for you to read. A grieving parent may experience just a few or all of these. They can even experience them all in one day.

❖ Shock/Disbelief

One of the initial emotions that I encountered was shock. I could not believe that this was happening to me! I could not believe that this was real! I had just come in for a simple test.

This shock was so intense that I was unable to speak for a time to answer the doctor's questions concerning what I wanted to do. My husband at the time had to make that decision. Many other parents likewise experience shock; especially if they were unaware anything was wrong to begin with.

❖ Overwhelming Grief

After the initial shock, and while still in shock, I began to just bawl. The grief was so overwhelming that I could not hold back the tears. My husband and I just held each other and cried for a very long time. After I cried all I could, the shock still remained.

When your child dies, you feel like a piece of fractured glass in many places that has just fallen apart into a million pieces. You don't think that you will ever be put back together again. That is how overwhelming the grief is!

❖ Anger/Rage

Eventually, when the shock of what has happened can no longer be denied and tears no longer flow, anger begins to set in. Sometimes, this anger can turn into rage. It can also be deflected upon others.

"[Sales clerks unfortunately often bore the brunt of my rage. Not sure why except that they were anonymous, and I didn't expect to see them again. I wish we could have the black arm bands back to identify us as grieving.]"
Anonymous

Likewise, I became angry at God. I became angry at those around me. Why was my baby not protected? I got so angry at God that I blamed Him. Following is one gentleman's viewpoint about getting angry at God.

"[It's okay to blame God and be mad. The only way you can forgive someone is to first accept you are angry with them. If you don't, the anger you feel will be directed toward the person closest to you. That's one of the reasons marriages don't survive the death of a child. This is where a strong relationship with God can mean the difference....]" **James W. Luff**

Furthermore, I began to question everything about my faith, about myself, and about those around me. And, not having the answers, it made me angrier. I wanted somebody to blame.

This was not right! A child was not supposed to die! I was angry with the whole world; especially those who did not want children and treated their children badly. Didn't they realize the precious gift that they had been given? How dare they treat their child that way or not want it! I would have given anything to have had my child back.

Anger is a very real part of the loss of a child. So, people need to be aware of this and not criticize grieving parents for it. Stuffing the anger does not help. And, as previously stated, if you invoke God as the reason for the loss in any way, it creates anger towards God. Then, the very one they need to turn to for healing, they will not go to.

❖ Jealousy/Envy

One of the biggest things that I had to battle with, and still battle today, is jealousy and envy of other parents. It is hard not to be envious or jealous of other parents who get to spend their lives with their children.

They get to do the fun things with them. They get to watch them grow up, go to school, graduate, get married, and maybe even have children of their own. They get to receive the love back from their children and to be honored or blessed by them.

For those of us who have never had any other children, we don't get that. Some feel left out. Although we may be happy for the other parents, we may become envious or even a bit jealous of what they have.

❖ Rejection/ Abandonment

Rejection or abandonment issues may arise after the loss of a child. Why? Sometimes, your old friends don't want to be around you anymore for some reason. They may be too afraid to talk about the loss; or, they just may not want to hear about it.

Also, after the funeral is over, grieving parents are sometimes left to deal with things by themselves. And, they may feel abandoned by people as a result.

Another area that this may occur is in activities. Parents with children often won't include those without children. The reason for this is that the children will play together. So now, the crowd that grieving parents may have been a part of no longer includes them. They feel left out and begin to battle feelings of rejection.

❖ Loneliness

Loneliness is quite a common feeling amongst grieving parents. Part of this has to do with the rejection/abandonment issue described above. Another contributing factor to the loneliness is when no other children or maybe even a spouse is not present. This makes the isolation even seem worse.

Furthermore, the grieving parents have time on their hands to dwell on the loss. This includes what they are missing out on with their child. It also includes feeling alone in your pain. Unless someone has been through the loss of a child, it is difficult for them to understand how the grieving parent is feeling.

For this reason, it compounds the feelings of aloneness. And, during this loneliness, it may feel as if the walls are closing in and about to topple on top of them and crush them. It is like a darkness that envelops them, and they can't escape it.

❖ Depression/Despair

Some grieving parents will experience such overwhelming despair that it will deepen into a deep, dark, depression. Basically, depression entails multiple feelings at the same time that becomes overwhelming.

Imagine for a moment being trapped underground with no incoming air, no way of escape, and no one that can help you get out. The darkness is the deepest that it has ever been. You may feel you will never see the light of day again. You may feel as if you will never be able to breathe again.

Although personally, I have not experienced this depth of depression, I know of others who have. However, I have been dealing with a long-term underlying depression that doctors state that they cannot treat. They have told me that I will always have it.

And, quite often, I've had people tell me that I was depressed even when I didn't feel like it. Additionally, I used to experience panic attacks for years off and on.

However, I remember God telling me during one service that He was my source of happiness. At the time, I was on an antidepressant that wasn't working. And, I was in such a daze that I could not focus on the message. But, I caught one key word. And that word was light.

In the Hebrew language, light means *"cheerfulness"* as well as *"light of day."* **(Blue Letter Bible/Strong's /Gesenius' Hebrew-Chaldee Lexicon)**.

Before the message, I had already been doing a study on this in **Genesis Chapter 1**. So, the verse in **Psalm**, which he preached on, that mentioned light, caught my attention briefly.

Since then, I have been able to do without medication. And, I am learning how to put my trust in God to overcome panic attacks. His Word says that *"[...He has not given us the spirit of fear; but of power, and of love, and of a sound mind.]"* **2 Timothy 1:7 (KJV)**

So, if you know of a grieving parent that is depressed, encourage them to get help. They may need deliverance from this. Allowing them to continue to be isolated can only draw them in deeper to despair.

❖ **Confusion/Lost**

Another emotion that many grieving parents may feel may be confusion. One may begin to doubt their belief system. This may cause confusion. There is nothing rational about a child dying in the parents' minds.

And, when trying to make sense of it all, confusion enters in. Many questions remain unanswered. If they are able, should they try to have more children? If not, should they try to adopt or foster children?

Which way do they turn now? What is their belief now? Who do they believe now? These are just some of the questions that may go through a grieving parent's mind. And, there are many others.

It is also for this reason that I do not believe it is God's will for a child to die.

His Word states that *"...God is not the author of confusion, but of peace,...."*
I Corinthians 14:33. (KJV)

Additionally, a parent may not be confused about the preceding, but they may be confused as to what to do next. They feel lost. All the plans they had for their child's life, what do they do with them now?

Following is an excerpt of **Nancy's** feelings after losing her daughter.

"[My heart is breaking. My heart feels empty. I feel lost. I feel as if an arm or leg has been cut off, and somehow I don't know what to do with myself. I am so scared of forgetting her. I am scared of forgetting her laughter, her cries, and her smell.]"
Fileccia / More Than a Memory / 99

Because the grieving parents are experiencing so many different emotional states and some simultaneously, it can become confusing. One moment they may feel like they are getting better, and the next moment something can trigger these negative emotions again.

They may begin to feel like they are falling apart again. Several have expressed that it is like their world has just turned upside down.

❖ Fear/Paranoia

Fear is one of the strongest emotions that I had. In fact, when I went for prayer, a lady expressed to me that God was going to remove my fear little by little. She stated that I had **A LOT** of fear. What was I so afraid of?

Aside from many general fears that people have, I was afraid that if I got pregnant again either the child would die or I would. Since it happened once before, what would keep it from happening again?

Additionally, since I had gotten angry with God and backslid, I had an **unhealthy** fear of judgment. I viewed my Heavenly Father as one who was standing over me with a whip and just could not wait to get me. Sometimes, even to this day, I deal with this fear. Although God is a loving Father, in my mind, I feared that He would punish me for anything I did. And, the punishment would be severe.

Others may get away with things, but not this girl. Even though I know this is untrue and irrational because *"... God is no respecter of persons:"* **Acts 10:34 (KJV)**, this is something I still battle at times. And, I believe it comes from the traumas in my life.

Truly, God does judge; but, my fear had become unhealthy. Instead of going to God, I would run from Him because of fear.

Another fear that I have as I age is growing old and childless and being left totally alone. Since I have no children to come visit me or to care if I were to get seriously ill, I battle with feelings of being alone. I battle with the fear of dying alone.

Fear is a spirit that can dominate one's life. It can turn into an obsession. And, it can cause panic attacks. So, it is important for believers to recognize this spirit and pray for deliverance for these individuals. And, it is important if they are a believer to remind them that God has given them *"... power, and ... love, and ... a sound mind."* **2 Timothy 1:7 (KJV)**

Furthermore, they need to be reassured over and over again that God is a loving God. He is a Father who wants to give us good gifts.

❖ Guilt/Shame

Some grieving parents may be dealing with guilt or shame. For me, this was pretty intense. As I recall, for several months, I did not want to be pregnant. After losing the child, I felt guilty. I felt as if my not wanting her at the beginning caused her death later on.

Also, I felt guilty for not being more educated on pregnancy. I should have known something was wrong, but I did not. I felt guilty for not seeing a different doctor on the day my appointment was canceled with my primary care physician. I felt like it was my fault that she died. Maybe, if I had seen the other doctor, she might have lived.

Furthermore, I felt guilty and ashamed for some of the things I said after she passed. And, some things were said by others that made me feel guilty for her death. Even though it was not my fault that she died, I still had to battle guilt and shame.

Additionally, I felt shame because she was conceived out of wedlock. Although I had tried to make things right and got married, the shame of my sin was still there.

❖ Sadness

One cannot truly express the magnitude of sadness a grieving parent feels. It seems to just linger on and on. Sometimes, it turns into depression. However, the sadness seems to remain there constantly. It is like an albatross around your neck. You feel as if you will never be happy again.

❖ Bittersweet Joy

This particular emotion usually occurs when recalling memories. Although a grieving parent may recall sweet and precious memories that bring joy, this joy is bittersweet. For, a memory is all they have left. There will not be any new memories to make. The child is no longer with them.

❖ Disconnection

When the death of a child occurs, a parent may disassociate or feel disconnected with what's going on. These parents may go into this during the shock phase. And, some may come out of it quickly. However, some may disassociate or disconnect from others or things for years. Following is one lady's experience.

"[I felt disconnected. I felt like my identity was taken away. I was always Stacie, Andrew & Cole's Mom. How could I be a complete person without being Andrew's Mom?]"
Sheila Auer-Jetmore

For me, after the initial shock and crying, I feel that I disconnected in some way. I could talk about my daughter and the death without tears. And, this disconnection carried over into other parts my life.

Although I could be accepted and loved by others, I have great difficulty in receiving that love and acceptance. I believe this is due to the fact that the great love I had for my daughter was smashed into pieces.

Additionally, I feel like I'm always an outsider wherever I go. I feel like a square peg in a round hole. And, as much as I want to be loved and to feel that love, I can't. I have had to disassociate too much of my life in order to get through. Although I am here in this present world and my rational mind knows it, I still feel disconnected, shut out, and a castaway at times.

There are a few times I will feel like I am getting that connection again just like a TV signal that will come in for a brief moment. But, it doesn't last very long. Usually, all it takes is one more hurt to feel unwanted, unloved, and disconnected.

And, mentally, I have replayed events over and over again in my mind as if watching a video. Although I go through my daily tasks and can function, sometimes I get a feeling like it's all a dream.

Unfortunately, some parents when they disconnect, they might not be able to do daily functions. For whatever reason, when the pain of a traumatic event is so intense, one may disconnect or disassociate. For some, this is a survival mechanism or coping skill.

❖ Distrustful/Betrayed

Trust can become an issue when one has lost a child. *"Can you trust getting pregnant again?"- "Can you trust the doctors to get you through another pregnancy?"- "Can you really trust others to tell them how you're feeling about the loss of your child?"*

And, for those who have been in church a long time, the question even arises, *"Can you ever trust God again?"* For me, this had been a very hard area for me. My faith and belief that God could do anything was sorely shaken.

One of the hardest questions that I could not answer even to this day is, *"If God is my protector, why did He not protect my child?"* That is the biggest thing that I lost when I lost my child, my trust that God would protect me from harm. I felt betrayed.

I know what His Word says. I believe His Word to be true. But, it is still difficult for me to exercise that trust and run to Him. Most people, in a crisis mode will run to God. And, it may be the only time that they do.

However, I find that I tend to run to God more when things are going well. And subconsciously, when things aren't going well, I tend to ask others to pray. I lack the confidence, sometimes, in God answering emergency or major prayers if I pray them.

Although I know this is not true, it's still stems from the matter of the ability to trust God. Sometimes, I still feel that He is punishing me when things go wrong. So, I have difficulty praying for myself but not for others in a crisis situation.

Other grieving parents may feel distrust or betrayal for various reasons. Following is a quote from my husband concerning his loss and feelings of betrayal during a previous marriage.

"[When I was on a trip--and I don't remember where--, I had noticed that my wife had a miscarriage. And, she had her parents to help her to dispose of the baby. When I saw the baby, it was about 5 inches; but, it still had already developed arms and legs. I was kind of shocked when I saw the event. I felt her parents didn't give the baby a proper burial. She didn't even ask me what to do with the baby. I felt betrayed.]" **Randy Sober**

❖ Hopelessness

Another major emotion that I deal with a lot is hopelessness. This hopelessness entails the lack of ever having children, the lack of feeling loved, the inability to feel love, the inability to trust God as I would like to, and of things getting better in my life overall. Sometimes, I would feel like I just wanted to give up on life.

But, if it were not for God in my life and eternal consequences, I probably would have. Hopelessness can lead to depression and eventually suicide if there is not intervention. For this reason, prayer is vitally important. And, it is also vitally important to have a relationship with God through Jesus Christ.

❖ Regret

This particular emotion my husband identified. Grieving parents may regret things that they have said, things that they did not do, or things that they have done. If their child was older, they may regret how much time they spent with their child. Did they spend enough time with them?

Regret can also include the things they won't have with their child. When you lose a child, you miss out on so much that could have been. And, this can cause feelings of regret.

For me, my regret is not taking a doctors appointment. Another one is conceiving her out of wedlock. Also, I regret not ever getting her a headstone or visiting the grave site more.

❖ Judged

Oh, this was a big one! I have felt judged and punished by God all of my life for that one particular sin and for those that followed after **Joy's** death. Sometimes, I feel like I'm being judged for every little thing I do wrong. And sometimes, I feel like it will not end.

God has shown me through the years that He is a loving God. He wants good things for His children. Yes, God does judge. But He is also a God of mercy and love. And, He gives a space of time for repentance.

Aside from feeling judged by God, I quite often felt judged by people. All of my life, I felt like I had been under such scrutiny by others. And, I felt like people had unrealistic expectations of me sometimes. I felt like I would never measure up in their eyes no matter what I did because of the emotional roller coaster I had been on.

❖ Unloved

Earlier, I stated how I did not feel love. I will never forget once in a service where I cried out to God to be able to feel His love. And, for a brief moment, I did; and, it tasted like honey! Many people say that they love me; but, I look for people to show me that they love me.

As stated earlier, because of the disconnection, it is difficult for me to feel loved. I'm constantly seeking approval from people as well as their love. Somehow, I equate that approval and favor as love. So, when I feel rejected, I also feel unloved and unwanted.

❖ Revengeful

As ridiculous as it may sound, revenge can be a feeling that some grieving parents experience. For some, it may appear justifiable, because someone actually hurt their child. But, for someone like me that had a stillbirth, it does not appear to make sense to feel this way.

Since I wanted someone to blame other than myself, I blamed God. I blamed Him for not protecting my child from harm or me from this hurt. So, as irrational as it may seem, I wanted to get revenge. And, the way that I did that was by backsliding. I dove headlong into sin and would not have anything to do with God for years.

But, one can never get revenge at God. It is ridiculous to think that we can. And thankfully, God is gracious and merciful. From what might be His point of view, I can see Him just laughing and shaking His head like a parent would at a child who is pouting or throwing a tantrum because they didn't get what they wanted.

❖ Indifferent

When one feels disconnected, indifference can become a part of that. A grieving parent may get to the point that they don't care what happens to them anymore. Because, caring only brings more hurt. And, although they may try to feel for others and what they're going through, it can be quite difficult.

For me, sometimes, I really want to be there for others and feel for them; but, part of me feels guilt and shame because I can't. It is like a spirit of indifference is there. Maybe, if I care too much, the worst might happen to them. For, whenever I seem to care for or about someone or something, it seems to get damaged or worse.

❖ Unbalanced

After I lost my daughter, I felt like I was out of balance. It seemed as if I couldn't get it back. I felt as if the rug was pulled out from under me; and, I couldn't stand up anymore. All my hopes and dreams were crushed. My world had been rocked. And, I struggled to regain balance.

And, sometimes my faith would waiver because I didn't know what to believe anymore. And, I went to extremes in my life: for example, shopping sprees, suicide attempts, etc.

Likewise, for some grieving parents, they may tend to go to extremes.

As discussed earlier, they may physically or financially take risks. Or, the other emotions may become extreme or irrational. It is very difficult to regain balance in their life when they've lost a child.

❖ Hopeful

Although hopelessness is one of the emotions a grieving parent often feels, they can also feel hopeful at the same time. As I recall, many times I thought that I might be pregnant again; and, I would hope so much that it would be true. However, at the same time, I was afraid it might be true. And, I feared that I would go through the same pain again.

❖ Emptiness

When grieving parents lose a child, it feels as if the bottom has just dropped out of their heart; and, there's such emptiness inside. They won't be hearing the child's laughter. They won't be hearing the pitter patter of little feet.

Everything that they would have experienced with their child is gone.

And, nothing of this world can fill that void. Only God can heal and fill that place in their heart again. Aside from their heart being empty, their home also feels empty.

❖ Unrealistic Intolerances

Some grieving parents may experience unrealistic intolerances. For example, one of my best friends says, *"that normal things such as the smell of her shampoo, or noise, or the whiteness of her clothes would bother her. She just cannot tolerate them anymore."* **Mandy Burkett** *(paraphrased from phone conversation)*

Therefore, what a grieving parent may have normally tolerated from you before the loss, they may not after the loss. And, simple everyday things may just set them off. They could be going along just fine for a while; but, something might trigger the memory of the loss. And, they become intolerant of you or a simple normal everyday thing.

❖ Suicidal

Sometimes, the grief can become so unbearable that grieving parents may have suicidal thoughts. I know for years, I had repeated attempts of suicide. But, after attempting it, I would get scared that I would never see my daughter again. So, I would go to the hospital for intervention.

Alma Collins Thomas conveys how the death of her son brought her to this point.

"[It was a long journey to healing. In April, it would have been his birthday; and, I considered committing suicide. I poured a bottle of pills in my hand. And, I heard a voice say, 'if you do this you will never see him again.' And, so after that I put the pills back into the bottle and was able to sleep the day away.]"
Alma Collins Thomas

As you can see, there are a wide range of emotions that grieving parents go through. And, sometimes, it can feel like a roller coaster ride. They could be up one minute and down the next. Or, they can be going along just fine and take a sharp turn for the worse.

One of my best friends, **Mandy Burkett**, says *"[that it is also like a car ride where the tires are just spinning along the road, and you seem to get nowhere.]"* **Mandy Burkett** *(paraphrased from phone conversation)*

In summation of this chapter, the following comment epitomizes initially how most grieving parents may feel when they lose their child.

"The day MY son died a piece of my SOUL died with him, and I have NEVER been able to go back to who I was before this happened."
Mandy Burkett

And, if you are a grieving parent, I hope after reading this and seeing the different stories, you'll realize you're not alone in your feelings and thoughts. God be with you!

When God Heals
Chapter 31

"The Spirit of the Lord is upon me, because he hath anointed me to preach the gospel to the poor; he hath sent me to heal the brokenhearted, to preach deliverance to the captives, and recovering of sight to the blind, to set at liberty them that are bruised,

To preach the acceptable year of the Lord."
Luke 4:18-19 (KJV)

"And I heard a great voice out of heaven saying, Behold, the tabernacle of God is with men, and he will dwell with them, and they shall be his people, and God himself shall be with them, and be their God.

And God shall wipe away all tears from their eyes; and there shall be no more death, neither sorrow, nor crying, neither shall there be any more pain: for the former things are passed away.

And he that sat upon the throne said, Behold, I make all things new. And he said unto me, Write: for these words are true and faithful." **Revelation 21:3-5 (KJV)**

After losing a child, a grieving parent may wonder if healing is ever possible. The answer is, Absolutely! However, Jesus is the only one who can do this for them. And, He may not do it the same way for everyone. Jesus will give you what you need in particular to heal. For me, it involved a move of the Holy Spirit at a ladies conference, a vision during prayer, a dream, and a visit to the graveside.

Furthermore, the healing may take some time. It can be a step-by-step process. I really like what **James W. Luff** said about healing for this type of hurt. *"[Lost my step son in 2007; healing is a process not a destination....]"* **James W. Luff**

Healing from the loss of my child has been a lengthy process. At first, it began by trying to go and hold other newborns. Then, I began investing in other children's lives and planting love seeds.

When I lost my daughter, **Joy**, I did not feel that I would ever have joy in my heart again.

But, I will never forget going to a church ladies conference once. I was fairly new to seeing the move of the Holy Spirit. And, my early spiritual upbringing did not teach on this. So, when I saw women on the floor laughing, I doubted that this could be of God.

However, one of the leaders got up and spoke and said, *"If you wanted to partake of this joy to come up and lay hands on these ladies."* **Anonymous.** Being skeptical as I was, I was going to go up and do it to prove that this could not be of God.

However, as many Christians do, we should not put God in a box. God does not always move according to the way we think that He will or by our agenda. So, I went up and laid hands on these ladies who were laying on the floor laughing. And, I will never forget the surge of joy and happiness that just overwhelmed me.

I began to feel so joyful in my spirit that I began to laugh. And, this continued for a good 15 minutes or so.

Finally, I was able to get up from off the floor myself. The anointing of the Holy Spirit was so strong. I could hardly stand up. I was supposed to be the driver home, but somebody else had to drive.

Beforehand, I recall as I lay on the floor laughing and unable to get up on my feet, another lady came up and placed her hand on my back. And, she prophesied over me. She said, *"That as I laid hands on others, they would receive joy."* **Anonymous.** This made sense. Often, in church, one will hear that your mess will become your message.

The next step of healing came when my pastor at the time gave me a book to read about **Theophostic Prayer Ministry**. And, he knew a lady who did this type of ministry. She is now my current pastor's wife. But, I remember going to her house, and during prayer, I had a vision. In that vision, I saw Jesus standing by my hospital bed **receiving** my daughter when she died. This brought me such great comfort.

Later on, I also recall having a dream. And, during this dream, I was at my grandmother's house in the kitchen. As I looked off to my left out the screen door, a young girl about the age of seven or eight came running to me saying, *"Mommy, Mommy!"* She was so full of joy. So, now I know my daughter is not only in Heaven, but I also know she's happy.

Ultimately, God brought such healing to my life and truly, *"... turned for me my mourning into dancing:...."* **Psalm 30:11 (KJV)**. Some wonderful and best friends that I have known for years decided to take me to visit my daughter's graveside in November of 2014. And, we had a wonderful visit. Previously, I had had such great difficulty in getting to the graveside.

After we arrived at the graveside, I asked them if they would take some pictures and give me some time alone. As I was spending time alone, I began to pray and cry a little. And, as I began to pray it turned into praise.

I had started thinking about all things that I missed out on, and that's why I was crying. I was telling God about these things. And, He opened my eyes to see all the evils of this world that she had also missed out on. And, He reminded me that I knew where she was.

My heart began to rejoice. And, I began to praise Him and thank Him. I did not have to worry about whether she would get saved and be in heaven for eternity, or locked up somewhere, or strung out on drugs, etc. I could praise Him because I knew where my daughter was.

Later, when I received the pictures, I noticed how the sunrays were shining down directly over where I was sitting and praying. For me, it was confirmation from God that He was with me there at the graveside. And, I believe that I have received my healing when I could finally praise Him instead of blame Him.

Following are some true accounts of other people's healing that they have received.

Alma Collins Thomas
"My friends being there, my family being there, and my faith in God helped me to heal. All I learned to do is trust and depend on Jesus, and to know that God makes no mistakes."

Anonymous
"[For 25 years, I have carried two truths with me all the time. (1). God is good, and (2). My son is dead. They can not be reconciled; but, they can and are both true.]"

Shirley Denton
"[After my children's death, I knew I had to save myself; so, I took up walking. It helped my stress. My first book was called <u>Tears of Sorrow A Mothers Journey</u>, and my second book is called <u>Healing Through Grief</u>. I chose to live and embrace life to its fullest and step out of my dark depression.]"

Nancy Feliccia
"I know that now she can see all the wonderful things God designed. I know she is walking without a cane, an elbow to guide, or a wheelchair. I know that sentences, words, and conversations are now flowing from her lips like

never before. And I know that she will forever be dancing and singing with Jesus." **Fileccia / More Than a Memory / 99**

<u>**Anonymous**</u>
"[I felt like God knew I was stronger than I thought I was. (Stillbirth and miscarriage).

The most helpful thing I was told, the thing that reminded me that there was life after stillbirth, was my husband telling me not to build a house in the Valley of the Shadow of Death. My goodness. It was like a light bulb went off in my head.

I could still grieve, but I didn't have to wallow in self-pity and loss. No. God didn't want that. He wanted me to trust Him in the valley, and take His hand and walk through that valley with Him.

Another very useful thing for me was reading the book of Job. It helped me to know deep in my spirit that God knew what was going on with me and had not forgotten about me. He knows when the mountain goats give birth (Job 37 or 38, I think); so, He was fully aware of my trial.

*Then, when I read **Job 42:5 (NIV)**, I felt like shouting from the mountaintop: '[my ears have heard of You, but now my eyes have seen You for myself.]' The* *loss of my first child (and later my second) drew me and others closer to God; and, I am forever grateful that their lives, brief as they were, were not in vain.]"*

<u>Teresa Pollard</u>

"[I didn't get mad at anything anyone said. Maybe, my case doesn't count though, because my "baby" was 27 when she died. The people who helped the most though didn't really say anything. They just gave me a hug.

I think people (doctors) need to give all the facts so that you can be prepared for the worst, but I'm not sure that I believe there is such a thing as false hope. Faith and a positive attitude can make a HUGE difference in "normal" outcomes. Kara proved that....

On the other hand, those who would foolishly declare a loved one's death as due to a lack of faith on your part (and there are some "Christians" who do) don't understand what real hope is. My Hope is in Christ, and the final decision is always His....

I don't have an urn. Kara insisted she didn't want "to be sitting up on a mantle with me staring at her all day;" so, I took them to a waterfall and spread them at the bridge near the bottom of the two mile hike.

*After my friend Krystal and I had hiked
up to the waterfall, we came back down
to find nine butterflies feasting on the
ashes. It was such an incredible symbol
to me that Kara wasn't really dead. She
was just transformed like those
butterflies into her heavenly form, and I
would see her again when my time
comes.]"*

Karen Stone Janiczek

*"[On December 25, 2013, at 6:50A.M.,
we get a call from our son, David, who
was calling from the hospital bed of our
one and only grandchild, Emma Faith.*

*"Mom. Come now to the hospital!"
"What is happening?" I asked. "Just
come…and come quickly!" And, he hung
up.*

*My husband and I dressed quickly and
drove to the hospital, all the while
praying in the Spirit not knowing what to
pray for.*

*As we put two steps into the hospital, my
phone rings again.*

*"Mom…Emma…went to be with Jesus."
I collapsed to the floor crying… "NO!!!"
My husband said to our son, "We will be
right up."*

*The hospital staff whisked us up to the
room as we both had tears running*

• • •

down our faces. As we entered the hallway, you could see everyone bunched outside her room.

As we entered the room, we saw our son sitting in a chair holding Emma…crying. As we came in, he stood up and gave me her to hold. (You see holding Emma was a rare occasion. I had only held her the week before for 3 hours.) It would take 3 nurses and my son to transfer her into your arms.

Before I go on, let me tell you about Emma Faith. She had a rare birth defect, called Omphalocele; her organs (small and large intestines, stomach, liver and spleen) were outside her body in the womb.

They found this out at 21 weeks and were told to abort the baby. But my son and daughter-in-law said, "no!"

Before we knew they were pregnant, my husband had a dream and saw a little girl starting to walk in our house. We were calling her Faith. My husband said, "Why are we calling her Faith? They will never name her that."

God told him we would have to have faith. And then, he woke up.

After we heard the news that she had this birth defect, my husband told them what God had shown him in a dream.
We all instantly started to call and confess that Emma was whole and healed. We had so much faith that we expected her to be born completely healed. But, she wasn't.

They did surgery after 1 hour of being born to put her organs back in--and then, another surgery to cover the hole where she had no skin. She had a few more surgeries for various things also.

Emma was on a ventilator her whole life along with a myriad of medications and other complications.

We had thousands of people praying for her all over the world. People we never met praying for her night and day. People called her the Facebook Baby, because that is how I would keep everyone informed daily.

We never lost faith that she was going to live a healthy productive life.

When Emma was 4.5 months old, the doctors told us she was doing great and to prepare for her to come home in January.

Emma had come so far, from near death for 16 days in her second month of life...to now coming home in January.

Everyone was rejoicing with us on how far Emma had come. They moved her out of the NICU and into a Ped's floor still having constant 24 hour one-on-one nurse just for her.

She was doing so well that on Christmas we were all going to get to hold her, some for the very first time.

Now, instead of holding her in life, we all got to hold her in death.

My son said that Emma was a gift from God, and it was a privilege to have her as long as we did.

Holding Emma now in death without all the tubes and wires was unnatural in a way. I gave Emma back to David, our son, and he instantly gave her to his dad and said, "Dad please pray."

My husband said later that he knew David was going to ask him to pray. He said, "I had no words, and the sadness was overwhelming." But, he prayed. And, part of his prayer was... "In everything give thanks, for this is the will of God."

Did we feel like giving thanks at that moment? No...but, there was nothing else to do!

A few minutes before 8 A.M., on Christmas, morning...our granddaughter was dead!

How do you call and tell people on Christmas morning? How do I post on Facebook and ruin everyone's Christmas?

All these people invested in Emma's life with prayer. Now, suddenly, she is dead.

The feelings and emotions that suddenly surfaced inside me...was utter devastation!

Christmas day...we came home and just sat and were numb--my whole family just looking at each other...while most of the world is celebrating.

That night when I got up to use the bathroom, I sat on the toilet and thought, "This has to be a dream?" And then, the sadness and grief surrounded me!!! I cried out to God, "Why God? We were all praying?"

And God said to me, "Karen...just keep praising me."

I paused, and then started to praise God right there in the bathroom. Did I feel like it? No, but there was nothing else to do. God told me to praise Him. I got in bed, woke my husband up and told him. We told our children, and that is what we did to get through Emma dying.

At her funeral, we had over 400 people attend; many came from hundreds of miles away. Why? Because, they were invested in her life.

She was the baby that changed so many lives. So many people told us that they had never seen more faith from us, and in turn, it gave them the faith to believe.

Why did Emma die? Only God can answer that…till we meet Him…I will keep praising God.

Oh footnote: My son and daughter- in-law now have a new baby Penelope Grace born December 19. Our Christmas was so blessed!

Now, when people ask us if we have grandchildren, We say, "yes…2…one lives in heaven, and her name is Emma Faith, and one lives on earth; and, her name is Penelope Grace." Because, we will always be Emma's Grandparents, or as we are known Pippa and Papa!]"

Written by: Karen Stone Janiczek: Daughter, Sister, Wife, Mother and Grandmother!

So, as you can see, *"... with God all things are possible."* **Mark 10:27 (KJV)**. And, that includes healing from the loss of a child. And, if you are a grieving parent, it is my hope and prayer that you receive healing through Jesus Christ as I and these many others have.

Conclusion

Undoubtedly, losing a child is one of the most traumatic experiences a person can have take place. It affects everything; the emotions, the spiritual life, and even the finances. Therefore, when dealing with grieving parents that have experienced this trauma, one has to be very careful.

Unfortunately, no right words exist to say to the grieving parents. Nothing that you say can take away the pain. However, what you say can increase the pain. Therefore, it is imperative that whatever you say to a grieving parent is scrutinized in your mind before you say it.

One thing that you really want to be careful not to do is to invoke blame upon God for any reason. It is vitally important that grieving parents be able to run to God during this time instead of away from Him. Don't be a tool for the enemy to use to put before them a stumbling block that would steer them away from God.

As you have seen in the preceding chapters, the best ways that you can help grieving parents are just by being there for them. This includes prayer, listening to them, talking about the death of their child even if it makes you uncomfortable, and doing things for them without being asked.

Furthermore, don't rush the grieving process. And, because the emotional state of the grieving parents can fluctuate so much for many years, you need to be prepared for the unexpected. Don't chastise grieving parents for their emotions. God will heal them in time.

And, don't expect parents to just get over it. As long as they are living, breathing, and have a good memory, they will never get over having lost a child. However, this does not mean that they won't be healed. It just means that they won't forget the experience and how the loss affected their lives.

When you pray for the grieving parents, you need to pray for healing for the emotions and for their broken spirit. If you are a believer, God has called all of us to pray. And, because it's a traumatic experience, there may be more spiritual warfare going on than you realize. I would recommend reading the book on spiritual warfare on the recommended sites page.

Finally, healing for grieving parents can be realized. True healing and deliverance comes through Jesus Christ by His shed blood and wonderful name. Drawing closer to God during this difficult time is the most important thing grieving parents can do!

And, a note for grieving parents:

As you have seen in the healing chapter, many have received the manifestation of the healing when praising God. When you get to the point that you can praise God in spite of your pain, it does several things.

First, it puts your focus where it should be. As long as the enemy can get you to focus on the lies instead of on God, he will keep you in that vicious cycle.

Secondly, it reminds you who is really in control. Although the enemy might have taken your child, God is already victorious over death, hell, and the grave.

"So when this corruptible shall have put on incorruption, and this mortal shall have put on immortality, then shall be brought to pass the saying that is written, Death is swallowed up in victory. O death, where is thy sting? O grave, where is thy victory?"
I Corinthians 15:54 – 55 (KJV)

Not only will God bring you through this horrific experience, but you will also triumph as you draw closer to Him and rest in Him. Just remember the promise given to those who overcome. We overcome by our faith.

"For whatsoever is born of God overcometh the world: and this is the victory that overcometh the world, even our faith. Who is he that overcometh the world, but he that believeth that Jesus is the Son of God?"
I John 5:4 – 5 (KJV)

Praising and worshiping God is an act of faith. It is how we exercise our faith. We just don't praise God and worship Him because everything is going great. We praise and worship Him because He is great and faithful to

His Word. This takes faith. And, when we have faith in Him and His Word, He will honor it.

One of my favorite verses of Scripture is **Isaiah 61:3 (KJV)** which says, *"To appoint unto them that mourn in Zion, to give unto them beauty for ashes, the oil of joy for mourning, the garment of praise for the spirit of heaviness; that they might be called trees of righteousness, the planting of the LORD, that he might be glorified."*

God has already provided for us during this difficult time. And, one of the things that He provided for heavy spirits is a garment of praise. Don't underestimate the importance of praising God, especially during this time.

Another thing that praising God does during this time is to witness to others. Many lives have been affected by watching people grieving the loss of a child, and they are praising God.

Aside from the stories in the healing chapter, I have heard others do the same. Praising God encourages and helps strengthen other people's faith. What greater impact and legacy could your child's short life have had than to be one to cause others to come to Christ or to have their faith strengthened in Him?

Although it may be difficult to do, take the step of faith and begin to praise God in spite of your pain. And, as I and several others have, you'll begin to see healing take place in your life. You won't forget the experience; but you will be able to deal with it a whole lot better. And, you'll be able to turn your mess into a message so that you can minister to others going through the same thing.

Lastly, I would like to leave you with some other poems that God gave me during some difficult times in my life. Hope you will be blessed by them.

P.S. I used to dislike poetry, but it was how God helped me express my feelings in order to heal. You never know how God will do it.

Abandoned Pup

Like an abandoned pup in a kennel,
I cry, "pick me-pick me."
People look down upon my level
not deeming me very worthy.
As the thoughts of loneliness rush in,
I realized that I was over looked again.

Then, one night I heard a faint voice,
"Why do you make loneliness your choice?
All these times that you've felt lonely.
I've called to you to choose me only.

You may have felt lonely,
but you were never alone.
I stretched forth my hand
and gave you a song.

People may have often overlooked you:
But, your name is written down 'tis true.
I have not forgotten you at all, you see
It is you that has forgotten me.

So, when you feel lonely or overlooked,
Remember my promises in the Holy Book.
I'll never forsake you, I know your name!
I'm Jesus-yesterday, today, forever the same.

Come to me without fear and dread.
I have my arms open to you widespread.
People will be human-that's what they will be.

But, always remember that "I am He,"
the one who redeemed you and has been by your
side.
I want you with me forever to abide."

CONFUSED?PERPLEXED? DISTRESSED?

Looking this way and looking that,
confused about which way to turn,
wanting direction where you're at,
all the while your mind doth burn.

Jesus did not cause this confusion.
Look to Him to stop the delusion.

REMEMBER IN THIS WORLD OF NUMBERS SOMEBODY STILL KNOWS YOUR NAME

Day by day, and year after year,
they ask for your number and you begin to fear.
Does anyone still know your name?

Yes, one does 'tis true!
The one that has created you--
Jesus is His name!
And, your problems He can tame.

Lord, Help Me Roll Over!
(picture a baby on the floor)

Father in Heaven, I love You so much!
Oh, how I long to feel your touch!
When I cry and wail in misery,
it seems that none heareth me.
Lord, help me roll over!

When I repented, I was able to see,
a little glimpse of Thy Majesty!
Facedown, I lie upon the floor,
your glory visible no more.
Lord, help me roll over!

As life's storms seem to threaten,
your voice to me doth beckon.
My eyes can only see,
the shadows cast about me.
Lord, help me roll over!

Although you say, "Child, here am I,"
day and night, I can only cry.
Although to you I may openly speak,
your spiritual language I do seek.
Lord, help me roll over!

I lift my head and hands to the sky
with fear and trembling, I know not why.
I long to seek and admire Thee,
fearing those who are watching me.
Lord, help me to roll over!

With each attempt, I continue to fall.
It appears that my back is to the wall.
Frustration and confusion bring much pain.
Succumbing to failure would not bring gain.
Lord, teach me to roll over!

The spiritual steps I must do
in order for my growth to be true.
Each trial that comes my way
will strengthen me day by day.
Lord, teach me to roll over!

When cometh accomplishment of this task,
your filling presence will remove my mask.
Future growth that I must face,
you will guide me at your pace.
Lord, teach me to roll over!

Your presence will make life easier to bear,
'cause my adoration of you I can share.
The Holy Ghost will guide me every hour,
And, I will know the full extent of Jesus' power.
Lord, teach me to roll over!

Worship and intimacy forevermore,
you desire now and on that heavenly shore.
Adoration and love to Thee I give,
forsaking all others for Thee, I'll live.
Lord, give me courage to roll over!

Power of Praise

Lord Jesus, we praise you for who you are.
We praise you in the house and in the car.
We lift our hands towards the sky,
for our redemption draweth nigh.

Our praise is not for what we see,
but for what we know you to be.
We praise you for what has been done,
for the death of the Precious One.

With your death our sin was forgiven,
not only that but you have also arisen.
You watch o'er us day and night.
Our battles you do help us fight.

We praise you always in everything,
clinging to the cross,
we know joy you'll bring.

We praise you with our
minds, hearts, and hands.
A joyful noise rings across many lands.

We praise you with instruments and such,
because we love you so very much.

When we praise you,
we enter your awesome presence,
and nothing else matters that is around us.

Lord, let not any pride, logic, or sin,
time, trouble, or feelings box me in.
These things could hinder my praise.
To You, my hands I must raise.

It's The Power of God

Each difficulty that I face,
God displays His amazing grace.
If to conclusions I don't jump,
Then, He'll thwart Satan with a thump.

When the bills pile up and the creditors call,
sometimes, I feel that there is no hope at all.
Then, God reminds me of the troubles of Jason.
in Thessalonica, the people were brazen.

They entered his house,
and took him and some brethren
before the rulers because of Paul's preachin'.

God was in control and so,
He said, "Let my people go."

When my forward progress slides
backwards a step or two,
I am perplexed and don't know what good
prayer would do.

Then, God reminds me how
Paul must needs fight,
a former battle for the Gentiles' right,
to believe in Jesus so they would be
able to live with Him eternally.

God was in control and so
They took His Word to and fro.

When I am persecuted for my belief,
I feel forsaken, my heart filled with grief.
Then, God reminds me of how
Paul and Silas one night
were imprisoned for preachin',
what a terrible plight.

As they sought God in that awful place,
He then displayed His amazing grace.
The ground did quake.
The bars did shake.

God was in control and so,
to the guard's house they did go.

When I am bodily or mentally cast down,
I feel like destruction somehow
doth me surround.
Then, God reminds me how
the people of Lystra groaned
And how, the whole city decided to
have Paul stoned.

The devil did not want that church to be strong
He did not want others to Jesus belong.

God was in control and so,
Paul, whom left for dead, arose.

No matter what burden I must bear,
I have a treasure that I must share.
It's the power of God and none of mine
in order that Jesus through me may shine.

Author's Corner

Sheila L. Sober currently resides in Arkansas City, KS. She has been married to her wonderful husband, Randy Sober, (pictured here), for the past six years. They have seen God do some awesome things in these past few years. Her husband has been disabled for all of his life with mild cerebral palsy, and in 2003, he was officially diagnosed with the same diagnosis as his dad. It is called hypoparathyroidism.

They have seen God heal bones, change x-rays, change his bone density for the better, and bring him back from total renal failure without dialysis. God is great and is their healer! Randy and Sheila still believe in total healing for him.

Sheila grew up in the Midwest, in Illinois, most of her life. Her wonderful parents took her to church and taught her well at home about right from wrong. Not having much else to do back then, Sheila spent a lot of time reading. Her parents told her that she had accepted the Lord around age 5, but Sheila could not remember doing so. Therefore, as a youth, Sheila made a decision to accept and serve the Lord.

Sheila began attending Christian school around junior high off and on. Because of her dad's work, they moved a lot. As a youth, Sheila was given her first **_Strong's Concordance_** by Mr. Bricker. It has been well used.

Some of the ministries that Sheila was involved in as a child or youth were: music ministry, teaching ministry, publications ministry, bus ministry, visitation ministry, cleaning ministry, and helps ministry.

Also, during her time as a youth, Sheila was offered the opportunity to learn more of the Word of God and earn two scholarships that she could apply to any Bible College. This was through the Word of Life verse packets. Although, she qualified for both scholarships after taking their tests, circumstances kept her from using them in time.

One of Sheila's favorite times as a youth was discussing scriptural beliefs with her dad. Often, he would take the opposite position and try to use scripture to back it up. She would do the same. Her dad wanted Sheila to know what the truth was and why she believed what she did.

Years later, because of the many churches that Sheila had attended because of moving so much, she became confused with some of the differing belief systems. Sheila had read in God's Word that He would teach you. So, she prayed and asked God to show her the truth concerning His Word. Immediately, He began to reveal to her His Word and His truth. The Word of God became more alive than ever to her!

Eventually, Sheila did finally get to go to Bible College online through **The Sure Foundation Theological Institute**. She finished her *Associates Degree in Christian Studies* and has plans to eventually complete her Bachelor's Degree and obtain a ministerial license. Also, Sheila attended the *Gladiator Camp* through **Perfected Love International Fellowship**.

Additionally, Sheila has an *Associate's Degree in Elementary Education* and an *Associate of Arts Degree in Office Technology*.

Furthermore, as an adult, God has allowed her to grow some more and to serve Him. Some of the ministries that Sheila has been involved in were: music ministry, publications ministry, drama ministry, teaching ministry, nursing home ministry, women's ministry, cleaning ministry, helps ministry, and occasionally the preaching ministry.

Sheila loves the Lord and has many different books that He has given her to write. She hopes to get them finished within the next few years as well.

And, Sheila has authored two puzzle books called ***Feasting In A Bountiful Garden—Word Search or Crossword Puzzles.*** They are available on Amazon.com

Sheila would like to leave you with this thought, *"Know God and His Word for yourself! It is very critical in these times!"*

Contributor's Corner, Recommendations & Citations

Recommendations

"Prayers That Rout Demons and Break Curses"
by Apostle John Eckhardt

"Deliverance Manual" by Gene Moody

"Please Don't Ask Me." Poem by Rita Moran

Contributions Corner

These are books, organizations, websites, businesses, or ministries of those who contributed quotes to this book. It is my thank you to them for contributing, and it is my hope that you will support them.

Businesses/Ministries

B&B Autoglass, Mesquite, TX.
https://www.facebook.com/michael.burkett.94
And
DJ Services, Mesquite, TX
https://twitter.com/djmikeblive
by Michael Burkett

"Kingdom Swag Magazine"
by Quitana Bailey

Tysean Thomas Friends And Family
Scholarship Fund
by Alma Collins Thomas

www.shiftedvisionministries.com
by Tammy McDonald

God INC. **Drs Michael and Karyn Janiczek**

www.nitpickingwithapurpose.com
by Marsha M., Copy Editor

http://Teresatalkstaboo.wordpress.com
by **Teresa Pollard**

http://candacekatestory.com
by **Nancy Feliccia**

www.arize-and-be-healed.com
by Patricia (Sistah Pat) Holmes

Books

www.DanceWithJesus.com
by Susan B. Mead

"More Than A Memory: The Candace Kate Story"
by Nancy Felicia

" Shifted Vision"
by Tammy McDonald

www.amazon.com/author/jwluff
by **James W. Luff**

"Tears of Sorrow: A Mother's Journey"
and "Healing Through Grief"
by Shirley Denton

<u>Works Cited</u>

Anonymous, Three. Personal Quote.
16-23 January 2015 &
14 February 2015.

Auer-Jetmore, Sheila. Personal Quote.
17-21 January 2015.

Bailey, Quitana. Personal Quote.
23 January 2015.

Blue Letter Bible. Sowing Circle, 2015. Web.
22 Apr. 2015.

Burkett, Mandy. Personal Quote & Interview.
16 January-21 April 2015.

Denton, Shirley. Personal Quote.
26-27 March 2015.

Fileccia, Nancy. *More Than A Memory: The Candace Kate Story*. Shreveport: A Journey Through Learning, 2014. Print and E-book.

Hare, Carol Estes. Personal Quote.
16 January 2015.

Holmes, Patricia (Sistah Pat). Personal Quote.
3 April 2015.

Janiczek, Karen Stone. Personal Quote.
2 April 2015.

Luff, James W. Personal Quote.
21-23 January 2015.

Maxwell, Diane Rev. *The Manna Principle.
V1-V5*. YouTube, 2015. 22 Apr. 2015.

May, Faith. Personal Quote. 16 January 2015.

McDonald, Tammy. Personal Quote.
17 January 2015.

Mead, Susan B. Personal Quote.
15 January 2015.

Pollard, Teresa. Personal Quote.
16-17 January 2015.

Smith, Rhenea. Personal Quote.
19 January 2015.

Sober, Randy. Personal Quote. 21 April 2015.

Story, Sharon. Personal Quote. 27 January 2015.

*The Rainbow Study Bible: Containing The Old
and New Testaments, King James
Version*. El Reno: Rainbow Studies, Inc.,
1989. Print.

Thesaurus: English (U.S.). Microsoft Word,
2003. Software Aid. 22 Apr. 2015.

Thomas, Alma Collins. Personal Phone
Interview & Quote. 15 January 2015, 15
April 2015.

Scriptures Used:

Genesis 1:28
Exodus 17:12
Deuteronomy 1:39
Job 1:1 – 12
Psalm 23:4
Psalm 30:11
Psalm 44:8
Psalm 50:7-12
Psalm 84:11
Psalm 86:7
Psalm 115:10 – 18
Psalm 116:15
Psalm 126:5
Psalm 127:3
Proverbs 12:18
Proverbs 13:12
Proverbs 14:5
Proverbs 18:4
Proverbs 18:21
Proverbs 20:27
Proverbs 27:1
Ecclesiastes 3:1 – 4
Isaiah 47:8 – 15
Isaiah 49:1
Isaiah 49:15-16
Isaiah 53:3-5
Isaiah 61:3
Jeremiah 1:5
Jeremiah 15:5 – 9
Jeremiah 33:3

Matthew 2:18
Matthew 4:1 – 3
Matthew 5:4
Matthew 6:19-20
Matthew 7:21
Matthew 8:7
Matthew 9:13
Matthew 11:28
Matthew 18:10 – 14
Matthew 19:14
Mark 1:40 – 42
Mark 10:27
Luke 1:61
Luke 2:14
Luke 4:18-19
Luke 6:38
Luke 11:13
John 1:12
John 5:19 – 30
John 6:39-40
John 10:10
John 14:1-3
John 14:23
John 14:26
Acts 2:17
Acts 2:42
Acts 4:10-12
Acts 10:34
Acts 15:36
Romans 8: 26 – 27

Romans 8:38-39
Romans 9:18
Romans 11:32
Romans 12:1 – 2
Romans 14:13
I Corinthians 6:19
I Corinthians 10:12
I Corinthians 10:13
I Corinthians 12:7 – 11
I Corinthians 12:26
I Corinthians 13:8a, 13
I Corinthians 14:33
I Corinthians 15:54-55
2 Corinthians 1:3-4
2 Corinthians 5:8
2 Corinthians 5:17
2 Corinthians 6:16-18
2 Corinthians 7:10
2 Corinthians 10:4-5
Galatians 1:4
Galatians 4:6
Galatians 6:10
Ephesians 1:5
Ephesians 1: 9 – 12
Ephesians 5:17 – 21
Ephesians 6:16
Ephesians 6:18
Colossians 1:9
Colossians 1:10 – 23
Colossians 3:9
I Thessalonians 4:3 – 7
I Thessalonians 4:13 – 18
I Thessalonians 5:11
I Thessalonians 5:14
I Thessalonians 5:18

I Timothy 2:1 – 6
2 Timothy 1:7
Hebrews 4:14-16
Hebrews 8:12
Hebrews 9:15
Hebrews 10:16 – 17
Hebrews 10:24-25
Hebrews 11:1
Hebrews 12:1 – 2
Hebrews 13:3
Hebrews 13:8
Hebrews 13:15-16
James 1:12
James 1:13
James 1:17
James 1:18
James 1:27
James 3:8
James 4:14
James 4:17
I Peter 1:3 – 5
I Peter 2:9
I Peter 2:13 – 17
I Peter 2:24
I Peter 5:8-10
2 Peter 3:9
I John 1:9
I John 3:1
I John 3:17
I John 5:4-5
Revelation 2:10
Revelation 2:17
Revelation 3:12
Revelation 4:11
Revelation 21:3-5

CPSIA information can be obtained
at www.ICGtesting.com
Printed in the USA
LVHW081112010222
709950LV00011B/256